ASPECTS OF
THE ADMINISTRATION OF
INTERNATIONAL JUSTICE

Titles published in the Hersch Lauterpacht Memorial Lecture Series

   I. S. Rosenne, *Breach of Treaty*
  II. F. Morgenstern, *Legal Problems of International Organizations*
 III. J. Dugard, *Recognition and the United Nations*
  IV. S. M. Schwebel, *International Arbitration: Three Salient Problems*
   V. T. Meron, *Human Rights in Internal Strife: Their International Protection*
  VI. I. Seidl-Hohenveldern, *Corporations in and under International Law*
 VII. I. M. Sinclair, *The International Law Commission*
VIII. C. H. Schreuer, *State Immunity: Some Recent Developments*
  IX. E. Lauterpacht, *Aspects of the Administration of International Justice*

UNIVERSITY OF CAMBRIDGE
RESEARCH CENTRE FOR INTERNATIONAL LAW

HERSCH LAUTERPACHT MEMORIAL LECTURES

ASPECTS OF THE ADMINISTRATION OF INTERNATIONAL JUSTICE

by

ELIHU LAUTERPACHT, CBE, QC
Director of the Research Centre for International Law,
University of Cambridge

CAMBRIDGE
GROTIUS PUBLICATIONS LIMITED
1991

SALES & GROTIUS PUBLICATIONS LTD.
ADMINISTRATION PO BOX 115, CAMBRIDGE, CB3 9BP,
 ENGLAND.

British Library Cataloguing in Publication Data

Lauterpacht, E. (Elihu)
 Aspects of the administration of international justice—
 (Hersch Lauterpacht memorial lectures v. 9)
 1. International Law
 I. Title II. Series
 341

ISBN 0-949009-90-3

©
GROTIUS PUBLICATIONS LIMITED
1991

All rights reserved. No part of this publication may be reproduced or transmitted in any form or by any means, including photocopying and recording, without the written permission of the copyright holder, application for which should be addressed to the publisher. Such written permission must also be obtained before any part of this publication is stored in a retrieval system of any nature.

Typeset and printed by
The Burlington Press (Cambridge) Limited, Foxton, Cambridge

IN LOVING MEMORY
OF
MY FATHER AND MOTHER

CONTENTS

Preface	xi
Table of Cases	xv
Table of Treaties	xxv
Abbreviations	xxxiii

CHAPTER I: INTRODUCTION   1

  A. Hersch Lauterpacht and the administration of
     international justice   1
  B. The subject defined   5

CHAPTER II: THE RANGE OF INTERNATIONAL JUDICIAL AND QUASI-JUDICIAL MACHINERY   9

  A. The increase in the number of tribunals   9
  B. Reasons for the increase   14
     1. The historical element   14
     2. Functional considerations   15

CHAPTER III: CONSENT   23

  A. Consent generally   23
  B. Rejection by the International Court of Justice of the need for a jurisdictional link in intervention proceedings   26
  C. The extension of the jurisdiction of the Inter-American Commission on Human Rights   30
  D. The quasi-judicial activity of the Security Council   37
  E. New approaches to compulsory jurisdiction   48
  F. Epilogue: Consent and State immunity   54

CHAPTER IV: ACCESS   59

  A. International organizations   60
     1. As plaintiffs   60
     2. As defendants   65

B. Individuals and corporations 67
  1. As plaintiffs 67
  2. As defendants 72

CHAPTER V: THE COMPOSITION OF TRIBUNALS 77

A. Party-nominated members 77
B. Chambers 82
  1. The ideal size of international tribunals 82
  2. The relevance of the distinction between arbitration and judicial settlement 85
  3. The approach of the International Court of Justice in the *El Salvador/Honduras* case 87

CHAPTER VI: APPEALS 99

A. Recourse to the original tribunal 99
B. Recourse to another tribunal 100
  1. Possibility of recourse included in the original settlement agreement 101
  2. Possibility of recourse arising from an extraneous instrument 104
C. Institutional provision for appeal 105
D. Whether a system of appeal should be developed? 109
E. Recourse against quasi-judicial decisions of political organs of international organizations 112
F. Appeals and references from municipal courts on questions of international law 114

CHAPTER VII: EQUITY 117

A. Some clarifications 117
  1. The meaning of "equity" and "equitable principles" 117
  2. The nature of the bodies applying equity 118
B. Modes of introducing equity into international adjudication 119
  1. By operation of law 120
    a. Treaty 120
    b. Customary international law 123

	i. Continental shelf delimitation cases	124
	ii. Compensation cases	130
	2. By reason of express request to decide *ex aequo et bono* or to formulate rules or recommendations	136
	C. Procedural aspects of the application of equity	145

Index 153

PREFACE

This volume is a revised and enlarged version of three lectures given in the Hersch Lauterpacht Memorial Lecture series in the University of Cambridge in November 1990. They were delivered as an act of filial piety in the thirtieth year following my father's death on 8 May 1960. The subject was chosen because – as is more fully explained in Chapter I – it lay at the centre of his interest in international law.

The Lord Chancellor, the Rt. Hon. Lord Mackay of Clashfern, presided at the delivery of the first of these lectures – a gesture towards Hersch Lauterpacht, this University, and the cause of international law which has been greatly appreciated.

These lectures were the fifteenth contribution (of which this is the ninth to be published) to what is, in effect, the second series, initiated in October 1983, of such memorial lectures. Previously, in the years more immediately following Lauterpacht's death, the then Whewell Professor of International Law, Professor (now Sir Robert) Jennings, had invited a number of prominent international lawyers to deliver occasional memorial lectures. Those who thus honoured Lauterpacht were Judge Philip C. Jessup, Judge Sir Gerald Fitzmaurice, Professor (later Judge) Richard R. Baxter, Dr C. W. Jenks and Dr Heribert Golsong. Regrettably, they did not present texts of their lectures for publication.

This book has been written near the opening of the United Nations Decade of International Law, during which much is bound to be said about the importance of improving methods of international dispute settlement. But the fact is that for all practical purposes the international community already has access to all the methods of dispute settlement that it needs. What it lacks is the political will to use them fully and consistently. Too often we hear it said that the commencement of international litigation is a step of final resort that should not be taken lest it exacerbate the delicate relations between the parties. In truth that risk is largely illusory. What makes relations between States difficult is not the litigation but the underlying dispute.

If negotiation, which is obviously the best method of settling differences, cannot lead to a settlement, then recourse to some form of third-party aid is clearly the only logical alternative. That said, the task is to improve the working of the present system.

Such improvement can be approached in two ways. One is by a radical reassessment of our attitude to the need for the consent of the parties for resort to international settlement processes. Now, there is no point in thinking afresh about something by reference only to the elements that have controlled consideration of it in the past. Proposals for a system of compulsory jurisdiction were advanced, and rejected, at the time of the establishment of the Permanent Court of International Justice in 1920 and again in 1945 when the Statute of the International Court of Justice was being drafted. But on those occasions the discussion took place only on the basis of general propositions and statements of dogma. The underlying situation of fact was that in 1920, and even in 1945, inter-State dispute settlement involving third parties had always taken place on the basis of an act of consent closely related to the particular episode.

Today, however, the factual underpinnings of the discussion seem to be changing. Though States still talk about the need for consent, in practice that requirement – at any rate when expressed in terms of *specific* consent – appears to have become markedly eroded. The strange thing is that the members of the international community, who have all participated – whether actively or passively – in this process, seem either to be unaware of the implications of their conduct or feel constrained to disregard it. It is, therefore, essential that the discussion should be resumed with a fuller appreciation that this so-called basic principle of consent is not, in fact, treated as quite so fundamental as has been assumed. Chapter III of this work, on "Consent", seeks to present some of the elements pertinent to this discussion. Of course, it cannot say everything and, in particular, does not consider all the alternatives to the present system. But it has been written in the hope that it says enough – and with enough supporting material – to stimulate debate and perhaps some movement in the right direction.

In parallel with a discussion of the waning need for consent, it is also possible to consider on a practical level some of the important features of the present adjudicatory system. Here, a willingness to look afresh at a number of underlying concepts – such as the proliferation of international tribunals, access to them, their composition and the desirability of an appeals system – could lead to material improvement.

PREFACE xiii

The same is true of the procedures connected with the ever-increasing resort to the broad and elusive notion of "equity". Treatment of various facets of these subjects fills the remaining chapters of the book.

I hope that I have succeeded in avoiding ideas that are open to immediate rejection as being excessively unworldly. Often, when about to curb the expression of some suggestion for constructive innovation, I have paused to ask myself the question: why should those scholars and practitioners committed to advancing the role of law in international relations suppose that there is lacking in the chanceries of States or on the benches of tribunals either the ability or the inclination to accept conclusions based on a critical re-examination of matters in the light of actual State behaviour or to shed past postulates that do not correspond with current realities? The contents of this book reflect my profound conviction that there is no good reason why we should make any such negative assumptions about the qualities of those who are in a position to enjoy the privilege of moulding the content of international law.

This may, therefore, be the appropriate place to recall the paragraph with which the last of the lectures concluded:

"To end a series of Memorial Lectures without even the briefest peroration would be strange. You will have noted that at no time has any attempt been made to advocate the merits of settling disputes by international adjudication. It has simply been assumed – as being beyond discussion and as being in the best interests of our international society – that a negotiated, but principled, settlement, or if no negotiated settlement can be reached, then the judgment or recommendation of a third party, is far, far better than the use of force. That is why, when gloom pervades, as occasionally it must, there is still virtue in attempting, by critical analysis and creative proposal, to promote improvement in the machinery of international justice. In the darkest days of the Second World War there were those, even in the highest places and most involved in the hazards of conflict, who were prepared to commit time and resources to planning for a future in which there would be less war and less killing. That is the spirit which must inspire us now. Though we may recognize that lack of resolve fully to put our evolving institutions to their proper use can ultimately destroy or render them ineffective, there can be no justification for failing to take every opportunity that may come our way to improve and perfect the international legal system. It is my hope that these lectures, delivered in memory of one for whom international law was the most precious of causes, may make some contribution, no matter how small, to our advance in that direction."

It hardly needs saying that the work is not a comprehensive study of the administration of international justice. That is why it has seemed right to include in the title the qualifying words "Aspects of ...". I am aware that on each of the subjects here discussed there are many more contributions to the literature than I have been able to recognize in the footnotes. Generally speaking, I have limited my references to items of which I have actually made use. A more extensive and systematic examination of the various facets of international litigation is in preparation and will, it is hoped, follow in due course.

This book has been read at various stages by some good, learned and perceptive friends who will know, despite the anonymity for which they have expressed a preference, that I think of them warmly as I pen these words of thanks. Their knowledgeable and authoritative comments have been most helpful. In the closing stages of the work I have had valuable help in the checking of the text from Mr Daniel Bethlehem, barrister, and Mr John Adlam. Miss Donata Rugarabamu has prepared the Tables of Cases and Treaties. Mr S. R. Pirrie, of the publishers, Grotius Publications Limited, and the printers, the Burlington Press, have been most helpful in securing the speedy production of the book. I am grateful to all of them – as well as to my secretary for thirty years, Mrs S. Rainbow, who has for so long deciphered my handwriting and put into legible form my paper-borne meanderings. Finally, I should like to add a special word of loving thanks to my wife, Catherine, for her constant encouragement and support during the preparation of this work, and to my children, Deborah, Gabriel, Michael and Conan, for their interest and concern.

Eli Lauterpacht

Cambridge
March 1991

TABLE OF CASES

A

Aerial Incident of 3 July 1988 (Islamic Republic of Iran v. United States of America), 105 n. 21
Air Transport Services Agreement Arbitration (United States of America v. France)(28 June 1964), 10 n. 12
Alabama Arbitration, 83
Alstötter and Others, *In Re*, 74 n. 26
Ambatielos Claim (Greece v. United Kingdom), 11 n. 17
Amco Asia v. Republic of Indonesia —
  Award on Merits (21 November 1984), 101 n. 8, 102
  Resubmitted Case – Provisional Indication on Jurisdiction (21 December 1987), 101 n. 8
  Resubmitted Case – Decision on Jurisdiction (10 May 1988), 101 n. 8
  Resubmitted Case – Award (31 May 1990), 132 n. 44
  Annulment Award (16 May 1986), 101 n. 8, 103
Aminoil Case, *see* Government of Kuwait v. American Independent Oil Company
Amoco International Finance Corporation v. The Government of the Islamic Republic of Iran, National Iranian Oil Company, National Petrochemical Company, Kharg Chemical Company Limited (Case No. 50)(Partial Award), 133-134
Anglo – French Continental Shelf Case, *see* Delimitation of the Continental Shelf (United Kingdom and the French Republic)
Appeal from a Judgment of the Hungaro – Czechoslovak Mixed Arbitral Tribunal (Peter Pázmány University v. State of Czechoslovakia), 104 n. 16
Appeal relating to the Jurisdiction of the ICAO Council (India v. Pakistan), 105, 143, 150 n. 92
Appeals from Certain Judgments of the Czechoslovak – Hungarian Mixed Arbitral Tribunal, 104 n. 16
Application for Review of Judgment No. 158 of the United Nations Administrative Tribunal (Fasla Case)(Advisory Opinion), 107 n. 26
Application for Review of Judgment No. 273 of the United Nations Administrative Tribunal (Mortished Case)(Advisory Opinion), 107 n. 26

TABLE OF CASES

Application for Review of Judgment No. 333 of the United Nations Administrative Tribunal (Yakimetz Case)(Advisory Opinion), 107 n. 26

Arbitral Award in the Dispute Concerning Certain Boundary Pillars between the Arab Republic of Egypt and the State of Israel (Taba Award), 10 n. 4, 77 n. 2, 149 n. 88

Arbitral Award of the King of Spain, *see* Case Concerning the Arbitral Award made by the King of Spain

Arbitration between the United States and the European Economic Community concerning Poultry, 12 n. 34

Argentine – Chile Frontier Case (Palena Case), 10 n. 5

Asylum Case (Colombia *v.* Peru)(Request for Interpretation of the Judgment of November 20, 1950)(Judgment), 100 n. 4

B

BP Exploration Company (Libya) Limited *v.* Government of the Libyan Arab Republic, 100 n. 4

Bank Bumiputra Malaysia Bhd. *v.* International Tin Council and Another, 66 n. 10

Barcelona Traction Case, *see* Case Concerning the Barcelona Traction, Light and Power Company Limited

Barcs – Pakrac Railway Company *v.* Yugoslavia, 137 n. 63

Beagle Channel Arbitration (Argentina *v.* Chile), 10 n. 9, 92 n. 41

Border and Transborder Armed Actions (Nicaragua *v.* Honduras)(Jurisdiction and Admissibility), 23-24

Brazil/United States Dispute on Processed Coffee, *see* Findings of Arbitration Panel established under the Provisions of Article 44

Buraimi Oasis Arbitration, 82 n. 11

Burkina Faso/Mali, *see* Case Concerning the Frontier Dispute (Burkina Faso/Mali)

C

Campora *v.* Uruguay, 64 n. 9

Case Concerning Certain Norwegian Loans, 3, 4, 94

Case Concerning Elettronica Sicula SpA (ELSI)(United States *v.* Italy), 88, 90

Case Concerning Gold Looted from the Netherlands, 11 n. 27

Case Concerning the Air Services Agreement of 27 March 1946 (United States of America *v.* France), 10 n. 12

Case Concerning the Applicability of the Obligation to Arbitrate under Section 21 of the United Nations Headquarters Agreement of 26 June 1947 (Advisory Opinion), 61 n. 2

Case Concerning the Arbitral Award made by the King of Spain on December 23, 1906 (Honduras v. Nicaragua), 104

Case Concerning the Barcelona Traction, Light and Power Company Limited (Second Phase), 63

Case Concerning the Continental Shelf (Libyan Arab Jamahiriya/Malta)(Application by Italy for Permission to Intervene)(Judgment), 27, 28-29

Case Concerning the Continental Shelf (Tunisia/Libyan Arab Jamahiriya) —
  Application by Malta for Permission to Intervene (Judgment), 27, 28
  Application for Revision and Interpretation of the Judgment of 24 February 1982, 100 n. 4

Case Concerning the Delimitation of the Maritime Boundary in the Gulf of Maine Area (Canada/United States of America)(Judgment), 88, 90-91

Case Concerning the Free Zones of Upper Savoy and the District of Gex (Switzerland v. France) —
  Order of 19 August 1929, 148-49, 151
  Second Phase (Order), 86-87, 137

Case Concerning the Frontier Dispute (Burkina Faso/Mali) —
  Requests for Indication of Provisional Measures, 89-90
  Judgment, 88

Chile/Peru Arbitration, *see* Tacna – Arica Arbitration

City of Tokyo 5% Loan of 1912, *Re*, 141 n. 72, 142

Commission of the European Atomic Energy Community v. United Kingdom Atomic Energy Authority, 61

Complaint by the Government of Ghana Concerning the Observance by the Government of Portugal of the Abolition of Forced Labour Convention, 1957, 10 n. 15

Complaint by the Government of Portugal Concerning the Observance by the Government of Liberia of the Forced Labour Convention, 1930, 10 n. 14

Constantine Case, 33

Constitution of the Maritime Safety Committee of the Inter-Governmental Maritime Consultative Organization (Advisory Opinion), 114

Continental Shelf Area between Iceland and Jan Mayen (Jan Mayen Continental Shelf)(Iceland/Norway), 10 n. 8, 142-43
Corfu Channel Case (United Kingdom v. Albania), 53 n. 65, 135
Cyprus v. Turkey (Application No. 8007/77)(Decision on the Admissibility of the Application), 59 n. 1

D

Delimitation of the Continental Shelf (United Kingdom and the French Republic) —
 First Decision, 10 n. 10, 125 n. 19, 127-30, 146-47
 Interpretation of the Decision of 30 June 1977, 100 n. 4
Disabled Peoples International et al. Case, 33
Dispute Concerning Filleting within the Gulf of St. Lawrence (*La Bretagne*)(Canada/France), 10 n. 3
Diversion of Water from the River Meuse, 118
Diverted Cargoes Case, *see* In the Matter of the Diverted Cargoes

E

E.H.P. v. Canada, 64 n. 9
Eastern Carelia Case, *see* Status of Eastern Carelia
Economy Forms Corporation v. The Government of the Islamic Republic of Iran, Ministry of Energy, Dam and Water Works Construction Company ("Sabir"), Sherkat Sakatemani Mani Sahami Kass ("Mana"), Bank Mellat (Case No. 165)(Award), 132 n. 46
Effects of Awards of Compensation made by the United Nations Administrative Tribunal (Advisory Opinion), 106 n. 24
El Salvador/Honduras Case, *see* Land, Island and Maritime Frontier Dispute
ELSI Case, *see* Case Concerning Elettronica Sicula SpA

F

Fasla Case, *see* Application for Review of Judgment No. 158 of the United Nations Administrative Tribunal
Findings of Arbitration Panel established under the Provisions of Article 44 of the International Coffee Agreement 1968 (Brazil/United States Dispute on Processed Coffee), 12 n. 33
Free Zones Case, *see* Case Concerning the Free Zones of Upper Savoy and the District of Gex

G

Ghana/Portugal Forced Labour Convention, *see* Complaint by the Government of Ghana
Goering, *Re*, 73 n. 27
Gold Looted by Germany from Rome in 1943 (United States, France, United Kingdom, Italy), 11 n. 20
Government of Kuwait *v.* American Independent Oil Company (Aminoil), 135
Guinea – Guinea-Bissau Maritime Delimitation Case, 10 n. 7
Guinea-Bissau – Senegal, Arbitral Award of 31 July 1989 for the Determination of the Maritime Boundary, 105 n. 18
Gulf of Fonseca Case (El Salvador/Nicaragua), 15 n. 43
Gulf of Maine Case, *see* Case Concerning the Delimitation of the Maritime Boundary in the Gulf of Maine Area

H

Headquarters Agreement Advisory Opinion, *see* Case Concerning the Applicability of the Obligation to Arbitrate under Section 21 of the United Nations Headquarters Agreement of 26 June 1947
Hirota, *Re*, 73 n. 27

I

ILO Administrative Tribunal Case, *see* Judgments of the Administrative Tribunal of the International Labour Organization
IMCO Case, *see* Constitution of the Maritime Safety Committee of the Inter-Governmental Maritime Consultative Organization
Imperial Japanese Government 4% Loan of 1910, *Re*, 141-42
In the Matter of the Diverted Cargoes (Greece *v.* Great Britain), 11 n. 18
Interhandel Case (Switzerland *v.* United States of America)(Interim Measures of Protection), 94
International Tin Council *v.* Amalgamet Inc., 66 n. 10
Interpretation of Peace Treaties with Bulgaria, Hungary and Romania (Advisory Opinion), 61 n. 2
Island of Palmas Arbitration Case, 83-84
Italy – United States Air Transport Arbitration, 10 n. 13

J

J.H. Rayner (Mincing Lane) Ltd v. Department of Trade and Industry and Others and Related Appeals; Maclaine Watson & Co Ltd v. Department of Trade and Industry; Maclaine Watson & Co Ltd v. International Tin Council, 66 n. 10

Jan Mayen Continental Shelf Delimitation, see Continental Shelf Area between Iceland and Jan Mayen

Judgments of the Administrative Tribunal of the International Labour Organization upon Complaints made against the United Nations Educational, Scientific and Cultural Organization, 106 n. 24

K

Klöckner v. Cameroons —
Award (21 October 1983), 102
Annulment Decision (3 May 1985), 102 n. 11

L

L.A. v. Uruguay, 64 n. 9

La Bretagne Arbitration, see Dispute Concerning Filleting within the Gulf of St. Lawrence

Lake Lanoux Arbitration (France v. Spain), 11 n. 16

Land, Island and Maritime Frontier Dispute (El Salvador/ Honduras)(Application by Nicaragua for Permission to Intervene)(Judgment), 26-30, 87-96

Legal Consequences for States of the Continued Presence of South Africa in Namibia (South West Africa) notwithstanding Security Council Resolution 276 (1970)(Advisory Opinion), 38 n. 41, 40 n. 42, 43-44, 45 n. 54, 46 n. 56, 53, 96

Libya/Malta Continental Shelf Case (Application by Italy to Intervene), see Case Concerning the Continental Shelf (Libyan Arab Jamahiriya/Malta)

M

Maclaine Watson & Co Ltd v. Department of Trade and Industry, 66 n. 10

Maclaine Watson & Co Ltd v. Department of Trade and Industry; J.H. Rayner (Mincing Lane) Ltd v. Department of Trade and Industry and Others, and Related Appeals, 66 n. 10

TABLE OF CASES xxi

Maclaine Watson & Co Ltd v. International Tin Council (No. 2), 66 n. 10
Mbenge v. Zaire, 64 n. 9
Military and Paramilitary Activities in and Against Nicaragua (Nicaragua v. United States of America) —
Jurisdiction and Admissibility, 23, 95
Merits, 18
Mortished Case, see Application for Review of Judgment No. 273 of the United Nations Administrative Tribunal

N

Namibia Advisory Opinion, see Legal Consequences for States of the Continued Presence of South Africa in Namibia (South West Africa)
Nicaragua v. Honduras Case, see Border and Transborder Armed Actions
Nicaragua v. USA, see Military and Paramilitary Activities in and Against Nicaragua (Nicaragua v. United States of America)
North Sea Continental Shelf Cases (Federal Republic of Germany v. Denmark; Federal Republic of Germany v. the Netherlands)(Judgment), 124-27, 135, 146
Norwegian Loans Case, see Case Concerning Certain Norwegian Loans
Nuclear Tests Case (Australia v. France) —
Request for Indication of Interim Measures of Protection, 18
Judgment, 18 n. 50, 26
Application by Fiji for Permission to Intervene (Order of 20 December 1974), 26-27

P

Pajzs, Czáky, Esterházy Case, 104 n. 16
Palena Case, see Argentine – Chile Frontier Case
Peter Pázmány University v. State of Czechoslovakia, see Appeal from a Judgment of the Hungaro – Czechoslovak Mixed Arbitral Tribunal
Petroleum Development (Qatar) Ltd v. The Ruler of Qatar, 81 n. 10
Phillips Petroleum Company Iran v. the Islamic Republic of Iran, National Iranian Oil Company (Case No. 39)(Award), 134-35
Portugal/Liberia Forced Labour Convention, see Complaint by the Government of Portugal

R

Rainbow Warrior (New Zealand *v.* France) —
  Ruling of the Secretary-General of the United Nations, 10 n. 11
  Decision of the Arbitration Tribunal, 10 n. 11, 74 n. 30
Rann of Kutch Case (India/Pakistan), 10 n. 6
Reparation for Injuries Suffered in the Service of the United Nations (Advisory Opinion), 62, 96
Report of the Advisory Panel on the Legality of a System for the Selective Adjustment of Quotas, 12 n. 33
Roach and Pinkerton, 32

S

Sapphire International Petroleums Ltd. *v.* National Iranian Oil Company, 136 n. 60
Selective Coffee Quotas Report, *see* Report of the Advisory Panel on the Legality of a System for the Selective Adjustment of Quotas
Société Européene d'Etudes et d'Entreprises *v.* People's Federal Republic of Yugoslavia, 136 n. 60
Sola Tiles, Inc. *v.* The Government of the Islamic Republic of Iran (Case No. 317)(Award), 132 n. 47
Sopron – Köszeg Local Railway Company *v.* Austria, 137-41
South West Africa Cases (Ethiopia *v.* South Africa; Liberia *v.* South Africa)(Second Phase), 19, 21, 63
South West Africa – Voting Procedure (Advisory Opinion), *see* Voting Procedure on Questions Relating to Reports and Petitions Concerning the Territory of South West Africa
Spanish Zone of Morocco Claims (Great Britain *v.* Spain), 83
Starrett Housing Corporation, Starrett Systems, Inc., Starrett Housing International, Inc. *v.* The Government of the Islamic Republic of Iran, Bank Omran, Bank Mellat, Bank Markazi (Case No. 24) —
  Interlocutory Award, 131-32
  Final Award, 131-32
Starways Limited *v.* United Nations, 61 n. 3
Status of Eastern Carelia, 61 n. 2

T

Taba Award, *see* Arbitral Award in the Dispute Concerning Certain Boundary Pillars
Tacna – Arica Arbitration (Chile/Peru), 137 n. 62

Thomas Earl Payne v. The Government of the Islamic Republic of Iran (Case No. 335)(Award), 133 n. 49
Tinoco Arbitration (Great Britain v. Costa Rica), 84
Tunisia/Libya Continental Shelf, see Case Concerning the Continental Shelf (Tunisia/Libyan Arab Jamahiriya)

U

United Nations Administrative Tribunal Advisory Opinion, see Effects of Awards of Compensation made by the United Nations Administrative Tribunal
United Nations Educational, Scientific and Cultural Organization (Constitution) Case, 11 n. 19, 96

V

Venezuela Boundary Dispute (Great Britain/Venezuela), 78 n. 5, 86 n. 22
Voting Procedure on Questions Relating to Reports and Petitions Concerning the Territory of South West Africa (Advisory Opinion), 3 n. 4, 93

W

Western Sahara Case (Advisory Opinion), 61 n. 2
Westland Helicopters Ltd v. Arab Organization for Industrialization, United Arab Emirates, Kingdom of Saudi Arabia, State of Qatar, Arab Republic of Egypt and Arab British Helicopter Company, 61 n. 3
White and Potter, 32, 35 n. 37
William J. Levitt v. The Government of the Islamic Republic of Iran, Housing Organization of the Islamic Republic of Iran, Bank Melli (Case No. 209)(Award), 133 n. 48

Y

Yakimetz Case, see Application for Review of Judgment No. 333 of the United Nations Administrative Tribunal

Z

Zeltweg – Wolfsberg and Unterdrauburg – Woellan Railways, Re, 137 n. 63

TABLE OF TREATIES AND OTHER INTERNATIONAL INSTRUMENTS

1794
Nov. 19   Great Britain – United States, Treaty of Amity, Commerce and Navigation (Jay Treaty) ....14, 83 n. 13

1815
Nov. 20   France – Great Britain Convention..83 n. 12

1827
Sept. 29   Great Britain – United States, Convention for the Submission to Arbitration of the Northeastern Boundary Question ....83 n. 16

1830
July 19   Argentina (Buenos Ayres) – Great Britain, Convention for the Settlement of British Claims...83 n. 12

1839
Mar. 9   France – Mexico, Treaty of Peace and Friendship ....83 n. 16

April 11   Mexico – United States Claims Convention ....83 n. 14

1895
April 1   Boundary Convention between Guatemala and Mexico....................70 n. 23

1899
Nov. 25   Protocol between Italy and Peru for the Submission to Arbitration of Claims to Indemnity..70 n. 23
             Art. 8 ....70 n. 23

1907
Oct. 18   Convention for the Establishment of an International Prize Court (Hague Convention No. XII)...115

1919
June 28   Treaty of Versailles (Treaty of Peace between the Allied and Associated Powers and Germany)
             Art. 304 ....67 n. 11

Sept. 10   Treaty of St. Germain (Treaty of Peace between the Allied and Associated Powers and Austria)
             Art. 256 ....67 n. 11
             Art. 320 137-39

xxvi TABLE OF TREATIES

Nov. 27 Treaty of Neuilly (Treaty of Peace between the Allied and Associated Powers and Bulgaria)
Art. 188 ....67 n. 11

1920
June 4 Treaty of Trianon (Treaty of Peace between the Allied and Associated Powers and Hungary)
Art. 239 ....67 n. 11
Art. 304 138-39

Dec. 16 Statute of the Permanent Court of International Justice 25, 27, 28, 90
Art. 36(2) 23
Art. 54(3) 148-49
Art. 58 148-49

1922
Austria – Hungary, Protocol 140

1923
Jan. 30 Treaty of Lausanne (Treaty of Peace between the British Empire, France, Greece, Italy, Japan, Roumania and Turkey)
Art. 92 ....67 n. 11

1924
Sept. 20 Italy – Switzerland, Treaty of Conciliation and Judicial Settlement ....11 n. 28

Oct. 30 France – Switzerland, Special Agreement submitting to the Permanent Court of International Justice for Arbitration the Dispute concerning the Free Zones of Upper Savoy and the District of Gex 148

1927
May 15 German – Polish Convention relating to Upper Silesia 67

1930
April 28 Czechoslovakia, Hungary, Romania, Yugoslavia, Paris Agreement (No. II) for the Settlement of Questions Relating to the Agrarian Reforms and Mixed Arbitral Tribunals 104

1944
Dec. 7 Convention on International Civil Aviation
Art. 84 105

Dec. 7 International Air Services Transit Agreement 105
Art. II(1) 143

TABLE OF TREATIES

1945

June 26   Charter of the United Nations 44, 45-47, 51, 107
- Chapter 1 .... 46 n. 56
- Art. 6 .... 44 n. 51
- Art. 24 .... 46, 48
- Art. 25 .... 45, 46, 53
- Chapter VI .... 37 n. 40, 46 n. 56
- Art. 33(2) 52
- Art. 36(3) .... 52-53, 54 n. 66
- Chapter VII .... 37 n. 40, 46 n. 56
- Chapter VIII .... 46 n. 56
- Chapter XII .... 3, 46 n. 56
- Art. 94 .... 59 n. 1
- Art. 94(2) .... 44 n. 51
- Art. 108 .... 21 n. 55

June 26   Statute of the International Court of Justice 3, 20-21, 25, 28, 51, 90, 91, 93, 94-95
- Art. 16 .... 20 n. 54
- Art. 20 80
- Art. 25 96-97
- Art. 25(1) 97
- Art. 26 96-97
- Art. 26(1) .... 88 n. 28
- Art. 26(2) .... 88 n. 29
- Art. 27 96-97
- Art. 29 .... 88, 97
- Art. 31 .... 77 n. 3, 79
- Art. 32 .... 20 n. 54
- Art. 34 .... 4, 20, 59, 60, 64, 66
- Art. 35(2) .... 59 n. 1
- Art. 36 95
- Art. 36(1) 52
- Art. 36(5) 23
- Art. 38(2) 118, 120
- Art. 61 .... 100 n. 5
- Art. 62(1) 26-29
- Art. 68 97
- Art. 69 .... 21 n. 55

Aug. 8   Agreement for the Prosecution and Punishment of the Major War Criminals of the European Axis Powers and Charter of the International Military Tribunal 73

1947

Feb. 10   Treaty of Peace with Italy .... 46 n. 56, 70 n. 23

TABLE OF TREATIES

Oct. 30   General Agreement on Tariffs and Trade 12

1948
April 30   Charter of the Organization of American States (as Amended by the Protocol of 27 February 1967) 34-35
- Art. 3j .... 35 n. 37
- Art. 16 .... 35 n. 37
- Art. 51e .... 35 n. 37
- Art. 52 34-35
- Art. 112 .... 35 n. 37
- Art. 150 .... 35 n. 37

May 2   American Declaration of the Rights and Duties of Man .... 30-33, 35 n. 37
- Art. I 32, 33
- Art. II 32, 33
- Art. XXVI 33

1949
Aug. 12   Geneva Convention Relative to the Protection of Civilian Persons in Time of War .... 33, 41 n. 45

1950
Nov. 4   European Convention for the Protection of Human Rights and Fundamental Freedoms 13, 107-8
- Art. 1 .... 59 n. 1
- Art. 6(1) .... 48 n. 57
- Art. 26(2) .... 108 n. 27
- Art. 26(3) .... 108 n. 27
- Art. 27 .... 108 n. 27
- Art. 28 .... 150 n. 91
- Art. 29 .... 108 n. 27
- Art. 31 .... 108 n. 27

1951
Sept. 8   Treaty of Peace with Japan .... 70 n. 23

1955
Aug. 15   Iran – United States of America, Treaty of Amity, Economic Relations and Consular Rights 133
- Art. IV(2) 130

1957
Mar. 25   Treaty Establishing the European Economic Community (*see also* Single European Act, 17/28 February 1986) 65

TABLE OF TREATIES xxix

	Protocol on the Statute of the Court of Justice
	Art. 51 ....108 n. 29
	Art. 54 ....108 n. 30
	Title IV ....108 n. 28
	Art. 177 116
Mar. 25	Treaty establishing the European Atomic Energy Community (Euratom) 143-44
	Art. 17 143-44
	Art. 17(1) 143
	Art. 18 143
	Art. 19 ....143 n. 79
	Art. 20 ....143 n. 79
	Art. 21 ....143 n. 79
	Art. 22 ....143 n. 79
	Art. 23 ....143 n. 79
Dec. 20	Convention on the Establishment of a Security Control in the Field of Nuclear Energy
	Art. 12 ....12 n. 38
1958	
April 29	Geneva Convention on the Continental Shelf
	Art. 6 129
1960	
	Statute of the Inter-American Commission on Human Rights (*see also* Statute adopted in October 1979) ....35 n. 37
	Art. 1 ....35 n. 37
	Art. 2 ....35 n. 37
Aug. 16	Cyprus, Greece, Turkey, UK, Treaty concerning the Establishment of the Republic of Cyprus ....41 n. 47
Aug. 16	Cyprus, Greece, Turkey, UK, Treaty of Guarantee ....41 n. 47
Dec. 13	Convention relating to Co-Operation for the Safety of Air Navigation (Eurocontrol) ....12 n. 40
1962	
Sept. 28	International Coffee Agreement 12
1965	
Mar. 18	Convention on the Settlement of Investment Disputes between States and Nationals of Other States 13, 69
	Art. 42 102
	Art. 50 ....100 n. 4
	Art. 52 101

1966
Dec. 19   United Nations International Covenant on Civil and Political Rights
           Art. 14 ....48 n. 57

           Optional Protocol 8, 13
           Art. 1 ....64 n. 9

1968
Feb 19   International Coffee Agreement 12

1969
May 22   Vienna Convention on the Law of Treaties 7
           Part V 7
           Art. 53 ....7 n. 11
           Art. 64 ....7 n. 11
           Art. 66 ....7 n. 11

Nov. 22   American Convention on Human Rights ....30, 34, 35 n. 37, 68
           Art. 8 ....48 n. 57
           Chapter VII ....34 n. 33
           Art. 41(f) ....34 n. 33
           Art. 44 ....34 n. 33, 64 n. 9
           Art. 51 ....34 n. 33

Nov. 29   International Convention Relating to Intervention on the High Seas in Cases of Oil Pollution Casualties ....12 n. 36

1972
Dec. 29   Convention on the Prevention of Marine Pollution by Dumping of Wastes and Other Matter ....12 n. 37

1974
Nov. 18   Agreement on an International Energy Programme ....12 n. 39

1979
Mar. 29   Canada – United States, Agreement on East Coast Fisheries Resources 90

Mar. 29   Canada – United States, Special Agreement to Submit to a Chamber of the International Court of Justice the Delimitation of the Maritime Boundary of the Gulf of Maine Area 90

Mar. 29   Canada – United States, Treaty to Submit to Binding Dispute Settlement the Delimitation of the Maritime Boundary of the Gulf of Maine Area 90-91

TABLE OF TREATIES xxxi

Oct. 31	Statute of the Inter-American Commission on Human Rights (*see also* Statute adopted in 1960) 34-35
	Art. 1 ...... 35 n. 37
	Art. 1(1) 35
	Chapter IV 34
	Art. 20(b) 34

1980

May 28	Iceland – Norway, Agreement concerning Fisheries and Continental Shelf Questions 142

1981

Jan. 19	Iran – United States, Declaration of the Government of the Democratic and Popular Republic of Algeria concerning the Settlement of Claims by the Government of the United States of America and the Government of the Islamic Republic of Iran 69-70
	Art. II(1) ...... 70 n. 21
	Art. V 132
	Art. VII(3) ...... 70 n. 22
June 18	Treaty establishing the Organization of Eastern Caribbean States ...... 8 n. 14
June 26	African Charter on Human and Peoples' Rights
	Art. 7(1)(d) ...... 48 n. 57

1982

Sept. 2	Agreement concerning Interim Arrangements Relating to Polymetallic Nodules of the Deep Sea Bed
	Para. 9 144-45
Dec. 10	Law of the Sea Convention 19-21, 51, 61, 71, 120-23
	Art. 7 ...... 20 n. 54
	Art. 18 ...... 20 n. 54
	Art. 59 121-22
	Art. 69(1) ...... 121 n. 11
	Art. 70(1) ...... 121 n. 11
	Art. 74(1) ...... 120 n. 6
	Art. 82(4) ...... 121 n. 8
	Art. 83(1) ...... 120 n. 7
	Art. 160(2)(g) ...... 121 n. 9
	Art. 161(1)(e) ...... 121 n. 10
	Art. 187 ...... 20, 61 n. 4, 71 n. 25
	Art. 235 72
	Art. 266(3) ...... 122 n. 14
	Part XV 19
	Art. 292 20-21

Art. 297(3) 7-8
Art. 312 .... 21 n. 55
Art. 313 .... 21 n. 55

Annex VI – Statute for the International Tribunal for the Law of the Sea
Art. 20 .... 61 n. 4

1986
Feb. 17/28 Single European Act
Statute of the Court of Justice (as amended by Article 11 of the Act)
Art. 51 .... 108 n. 29
Art. 54 .... 108 n. 30
Title IV .... 108 n. 28

Sept. 11 Egypt – Israel, Arbitration Compromis
Art. IX .... 8 n. 14, 77 n. 2

ABBREVIATIONS

AJIL	*American Journal of International Law*
American Convention	American Convention on Human Rights, 1969
American Declaration	American Declaration of the Rights and Duties of Man, 1948
Annuaire	*Annuaire de l'Institut de Droit International*
Basic Documents	OAS, *Basic Documents Pertaining to Human Rights in the Inter-American System* (updated to 1 March 1988), OEA/Ser. L.V./11.71, Doc. 6 rev. 1
BYIL	*British Yearbook of International Law*
DUSPIL	*Digest of United States Practice in International Law*
EEC	European Economic Community
Hague Recueil	*Recueil des Cours* of The Hague Academy of International Law
Hudson, *PCIJ*	Hudson, *The Permanent Court of International Justice, 1920-1942 (1943)*
IACHR	Inter-American Commission on Human Rights
ICC	International Chamber of Commerce
ICJ	International Court of Justice
ICSID	International Centre for the Settlement of Investment Disputes
ICSID Convention	ICSID Convention on the Settlement of Disputes between States and Nationals of other States, 1966
ICSID Review	*ICSID Review – Foreign Investment Law Journal*
ILC	International Law Commission
ILM	*International Legal Materials*
ILO	International Labour Organization
ILR	*International Law Reports* (including also the *Annual Digest and Reports of Public International Law Cases*, the title under which the first 16 volumes of the series were published.)

INGOs	International non-governmental organizations
Iran-US CTR	*Iran-United States Claims Tribunal Reports* (Volume 1 was published in 1983 and the series now extends to 23 volumes.)
LNOJ	*League of Nations, Official Journal*
LOS	Law of the Sea
MAT	Mixed Arbitral Tribunal
Moore	Moore, *History and Digest of the International Arbitrations to which the United States has been a Party* (1898, in six volumes)
OAS	Organization of American States
O-F & W	Oellers-Frahm and Wühler, *Dispute Settlement in Public International Law, Texts and Materials* (1984)
PCIJ	Permanent Court of International Justice
Rosenne, *ICJ*	Rosenne, *The Law and Procedure of the International Court of Justice*, 2nd ed.
UN	United Nations
UNESCO	UN Educational, Scientific and Cultural Organization
UNRIAA	*United Nations Reports of International Arbitral Awards*
YBCA	*Yearbook Commercial Arbitration*
YBICJ	*Yearbook of the International Court of Justice*
YBILC	*Yearbook of the ILC*

CHAPTER I

INTRODUCTION

A. HERSCH LAUTERPACHT AND THE ADMINISTRATION OF INTERNATIONAL JUSTICE

At every stage of his career, academic and eventually judicial, Lauterpacht was deeply concerned with the possibilities and problems of the settlement of international disputes by third parties. His first monograph, on *Private Law Sources and Analogies of International Law*, published in 1927, though not dealing with the procedure of adjudication, sought to demonstrate the ability of international tribunals to find suitable answers to all substantive questions no matter how sparse might be the quantity of established international law on the subject. By a careful review of arbitral and judicial decisions over the previous century he showed how international tribunals had been able to overcome the scarcity of specific precedents by the application of general principles of law derived from the principal national legal systems.

Lauterpacht further proclaimed his belief in the efficacy of the judicial settlement of international disputes in his second major study, *The Function of Law in the International Community*, published in 1933. The fundamental theme of this now classic work was the capacity, at any rate in theoretical terms, of international courts to resolve any and every type of issue that might give rise to contention between States. There was, in his view, no such thing as a non-justiciable issue, that is, an issue inherently incapable of being resolved in legal terms. He rejected the view that there are issues too important to be resolved simply in accordance with law. However, although he recognized that the structure and content of international relations would require occasional change, it seems that he significantly underestimated how extensive and constant that need would become. In arguing that its true dimensions had been distorted by other writers, he said "The principal of these reasons is the fact that, in international relations, the main source of the conditions calling for change is obsolete or unjust rights of individual States grounded in contractual agreements of indefinite duration based on force".[1] His thesis was that "most so-called conflicts of interests are due, not to economic necessities, but to the imperfections of international legal organization, in particular to the legal admissibility of force and the absence of judicial settlement".[2] Evidently, at that time he did not foresee, indeed he could not have foreseen, the immense pressures for change that were to be occasioned by the emergence over the next three decades of a host of new States; nor could he then have conceived the extent to which economic factors would, even within two decades, have attained such prominence that a large part of international cooperative activity since the Second World War has been taken up with the development and implementation of new international economic arrangements, not least in such central areas as the law of the sea and international environmental law. But these limitations in his prophetic ability only marginally affect the validity of his central theme; they certainly do not undermine it. International adjudication remains for us, as it was for him, a fundamental element in the international legal system.

Lauterpacht's view of the dominant role of international tribunals is reflected in two of the remaining three of his major monographs. First, in 1934 he published *The Development of International Law by the Permanent Court of International Justice*, of which a second and much more substantial edition was to appear in 1958.[3] Here his devotion to judicial settlement is demonstrated by a vigorous, critical and at the same time constructive analysis of the Court's impact on the substance of international law.

The second work contributed to the development of international adjudication in a different way. In 1945 he

---

[1] *Function of Law*, 248.
[2] *Ibid.*, 250.
[3] Under the title of *The Development of International Law by the International Court*.

published *An International Bill of the Rights of Man*, a seminal work in this field. Here, in his endeavour to formulate an effective system for the international protection of human rights, Lauterpacht necessarily had to start with a detailed study of the place of the individual as a subject of international law. This was more fully worked out in the second edition which appeared in 1950 under the title *International Law and Human Rights*. In particular, he demonstrated, in a chapter on the "international procedural capacity of individuals", that the provision in the Statute of the ICJ that "only States may be parties to disputes before the Court" was not a declaration of an immutable state of affairs in international adjudication but only a provision peculiar to the operation of that particular tribunal. If States were prepared to accord procedural capacity to individuals, that was a status which international law could readily absorb. He also discussed the place of judicial machinery in the implementation of human rights standards.

There remains one further and important context in which Lauterpacht's interest in the administration of justice was strongly demonstrated. This was as a judge of the ICJ – a position that he held from 1955 until his death in 1960. His best known contribution during that period was his separate opinion in the *Case Concerning Certain Norwegian Loans*[4] in which he objected, on fundamental principle, to a declaration in which a State, purportedly accepting the Court's jurisdiction, reserved the right to determine after proceedings had been commenced that the Court should not exercise jurisdiction. He regarded such a reservation as being inconsistent with the right accorded to the Court by the Statute to be the judge of its own jurisdiction and, therefore, in his view both the reservation, and the declaration of which it formed part, were invalid. Although it must remain an open question whether Lauterpacht's view would then have

---

[4] *ICJ Reports 1957*, 9, 24 *ILR* 782. See also p. 94 below. Lauterpacht's separate opinion on *South-West Africa – Voting Procedure, ICJ Reports 1955*, 67, 22 *ILR* 651, which dealt amongst other matters with the effect of resolutions of the General Assembly, was also influential.

commended itself to the Court as a whole or would do so today,[5] the commitment that he thus demonstrated to the role of the Court, and the terms in which he expressed it, made a profound impression. In due course, a number of States that had included in their declarations reservations similar to the one made by France withdrew the offending reservations, being concerned evidently that their declarations might otherwise be regarded as tainted by invalidity.

Finally, there is another product of Lauterpacht's time on the Court that is still virtually unknown. In September 1955, that is to say, within about seven months of his taking his seat on the bench, Lauterpacht submitted to his fellow judges a "Provisional Report on the Revision of the Statute of the Court". In this text, of some 104 typewritten pages, which is an internal document of the Court, Lauterpacht favoured the abolition of the institution of *ad hoc* judges, expressed doubts (later elaborated in his separate opinion in the *Norwegian Loans* case)[6] regarding the validity of "automatic" reservations, raised the question of conferring on the Court compulsory jurisdiction in respect of disputes involving the interpretation and application of treaties, proposed that either the Court's indication of interim measures of protection should be made binding or that that faculty should be completely abolished, urged that the Court might be empowered to add to its legally binding judgment non-binding recommendations as to changes in the law that its consideration of the particular case might suggest as being desirable, reverted to his earlier proposal that the Court be empowered to give advisory opinions on points of customary international law referred to it by national courts, and proposed amendment of Article 34 of the Statute so as to allow

---

[5] In its judgment, the Court dealt with the point as follows:
"The Court does not consider that it should examine whether the French reservation is consistent with the undertaking of a legal obligation and is compatible with Art. 36, paragraph 6, of the Statute . . . The validity of the reservation has not been questioned by the Parties. It is clear that France fully maintains its Declaration, including the reservation, and that Norway relies upon the reservation." (*ICJ Reports 1957*, 26-27, 24 *ILR* 789)
[6] See above, p. 3 and below, p. 94.

international organizations and individuals to become parties to disputes before the Court.[7]

It is, therefore, entirely proper to pay tribute to the memory of this distinguished scholar and judge by re-entering a field that was not only central to his own work but is also one which is fundamental to the promotion and maintenance of order in the international society in which we live. No matter how sharp the division between those, such as Lauterpacht, who saw no limit to the utility of courts in the international system, and those, such as Westlake, one of Lauterpacht's predecessors as Whewell Professor at Cambridge, who did not go so far, no one has ever suggested that there is no place in the organized society of States for the judicial settlement of disputes. In measuring the role of international adjudication one must bear in mind not merely the actual use made of judicial and arbitral instruments; one must also take into account the ever increasing demonstration by States of their willingness to accord a role to such machinery – a willingness shown not only by the repeated inclusion in treaties, both bilateral and multilateral, of clauses conferring compulsory jurisdiction upon tribunals, whether the ICJ or other more specialized systems of settlement, but also by participation in the developing system of jurisdiction based on more remote acts of consent.[8]

B. THE SUBJECT DEFINED

Having thus recalled the extent of Lauterpacht's commitment to the subject, it may be well before proceeding further to identify more precisely what is meant by "the administration of international justice". From the manner in which Lauterpacht's interest has been described, it will be seen that we are not here concerned with "justice" in the broadest sense of the term – of

---

[7] The document has not yet been published, but the permission of the Court has been obtained for its publication in Lauterpacht's *Collected Papers*. Its place is in the fifth volume of that series – a volume of which the editing has not yet been completed. My regret at that editorial delay is increased by this recollection of the document's continuing and contemporary interest.
[8] See below, Ch. III.

what is right and wrong and of how society should frame its laws with a view to the satisfactory achievement of the most desirable community objectives. It goes without saying that the examination of such questions would be important. It is, however, something that can only be pursued either in great detail in relation to specific problems or on a highly generalized plane. Neither approach appears suitable for these lectures.[9] They will, instead, be limited to problems of international justice on a different plane, namely, the methods and institutions that States use in the litigious settlement of disputes. If one may apply to international law the traditional division of the machinery of government into the three branches, legislative, executive and judicial, our interest lies principally in the judicial branch of the international system.

However, in adopting the administration of international adjudication as the subject of these lectures, it is essential to stress that litigation is not the only, or even the best, way of settling disputes. It is an inescapable fact that issues that divide States are best settled by negotiation and agreement. That is true whether the dispute is one that falls to be resolved within the framework of existing law or is one of such novelty or proportions that a specifically legislative effort is called for. The greater the direct involvement of the opposing parties in the process of finding a solution to their differences, the greater the likelihood of a satisfactory and lasting outcome. That is why, in the traditional presentation of methods of international dispute settlement, negotiation comes first, followed by the associated and, at their margins, the closely interconnected concepts of good offices, mediation and conciliation.

But just as these latter concepts merge into one another so, as we shall presently see, there is a tendency for them to spill over into the process that we tend to think of as judicial settlement. We

---

[9] One's hesitation to enter into this field is increased by the appearance of Philip Allott's substantial and stimulating contribution, *Eunomia* (1990). This exposition of the new order of international society on a philosophic plane is bound to make a profound impression on every reader and the essentials of its thinking are ones that international lawyers must take into account.

must not, in approaching this subject, assume that the administration of justice in the international field requires either that the tribunal must strictly apply a pre-established and immutable set of rules or that the decision of the tribunal must necessarily be one that is binding on the parties. In the first respect, as will be shown later in the discussion on the role and application of equity, there are a number of central areas of international interest in which tribunals are required to apply "equity" or something other than established rules of law.[10] In the second respect, we must acknowledge a lack of congruity – one of many – in the analogy that we are inclined to draw between the law operating between States and the law operating between the subjects of the law within the State: whereas within the sphere of national judicial settlement the qualities of "application of the *law*" and of "*binding* character" are to a high degree associated with the judgment of a court, the international community has come to recognize two things: first, that a determination by a third party, even though it may not be founded in pre-existing law, can represent an important discharge of the judicial function; and, second, that the existence of, and if possible the obligation to use, a third party settlement process is important even if the outcome of that process is not formally binding. As a result, provisions for conciliation have appeared in a number of important instruments. The Vienna Convention on the Law of Treaties, 1969, though containing no general mechanism for the settlement of disputes relating to treaties or even to its own interpretation, introduces conciliation as the procedure for resolving differences arising under Part V (Invalidity, Termination and Suspension of the Operation of Treaties).[11] Again, one of the specially significant contributions made by the 1982 Law of the Sea Convention to the structure of international dispute settlement is the concept of "compulsory conciliation", developed as a replacement of compulsory judicial settlement, of

---

[10] See below, Ch. VII.
[11] Art. 66. There is an exception for disputes concerning the application or interpretation of Arts. 53 or 64 (relating to *jus cogens*). After the lapse of the stipulated period, these may be submitted to the ICJ.

disputes arising out of the exercise by a coastal State of its rights in relation to the conservation and management of living resources in its exclusive economic zone.[12] Such conciliation does not lead to a binding decision. Yet again, an important function is performed by the UN Human Rights Committee, under the Optional Protocol to the International Covenant on Civil and Political Rights, even though the outcome of its consideration of a complaint is not a binding judgment but only an expression of "views"[13] which commits neither side to remedial action.[14]

In short, our concern here is not simply with tribunals that apply law and reach binding judgments. Our interest extends also to the identification and consideration of a range of contentious situations characterized by the fact that one party is enabled to present a case to a third person in order to obtain a conclusion, whether it be a judgment or merely a view or a recommendation, which, whether for legal or other reasons, is likely to influence the conduct of the other party in a constructive way.

---

[12] Law of the Sea Convention 1982, Art. 297(3).

[13] For "views" expressed by the Committee in various cases, see *ILR* volumes 62, 68, 69, 70, 71, 78 and 79, and UN Human Rights Committee, *Selected Decisions under the Optional Protocol*, vols. 1 and 2, UN docs. CCPR/C/OP/1 and 2 (1985 and 1990). See also below, p. 13.

[14] The continuing and lively interest in conciliation may be illustrated by at least three examples:
(i) in specific terms, by Art. IX of the Arbitration Agreement between Egypt and Israel of 11 September 1986, relating to the boundary in the Sinai and at Taba, which provided for a conciliation procedure to operate in parallel with part of the arbitration process. This conciliation process was unsuccessful and the arbitration continued. Art. IX is reproduced in the Award, 80 *ILR* 226, at 243. See also comment by E. Lauterpacht in "The Taba Case: Some Recollections and Reflections", 23 *Israel Law Review* 443, at 452 (1989);
(ii) in general terms, by the initiative taken by Guatemala at the UN General Assembly, 1990 on "Conciliation Rules of the United Nations", UN doc. A/45/143, 16 July 1990. Art. 39 of the proposed Rules has a particular bearing on the process used in the *Taba* case just mentioned;
(iii) and, also in general terms, the whole approach in the domestic legal sphere to "alternative dispute resolution", the applicability of which to international differences calls for consideration.

Another example of provision for compulsory conciliation is to be found in the dispute settlement procedure of the Organization of Eastern Caribbean States, Treaty of 18 June 1981. The text is printed in the valuable collection of material providing for the judicial and arbitral settlement of disputes compiled by Oellers-Frahm and Wühler, *Dispute Settlement in Public International Law, Texts and Materials* (1984) (hereinafter O-F & W), 148.

CHAPTER II

THE RANGE OF INTERNATIONAL JUDICIAL AND QUASI-JUDICIAL MACHINERY

A. THE INCREASE IN THE NUMBER OF TRIBUNALS

In attempting an assessment of some aspects of the present administration of international justice, it is proper to begin with a consideration of the present range of international judicial machinery. The purpose of this review is not merely descriptive, though it does no harm to remind ourselves of the remarkable amount of international activity that falls within judicial or arbitral purview. It is rather to enable us to enquire how we have reached our present situation, whether it is the best thing that could have happened and whether we should seek to improve the system in any way.

Although the ICJ is described as "the principal judicial organ" of the UN and the UN is the largest and most comprehensive of international organizations, it remains a fact that, in their practical approach to the administration of international justice, States have by no means limited themselves to the ICJ. Today we find important areas of contention involving States that are allocated to other tribunals.

First, it may be noted that many disputes of a kind that could have been submitted to the ICJ, in the sense that they were straightforward inter-State disputes relating to the application of treaties or to questions of customary international law, have since 1945 (the date of the establishment of the ICJ)[1] been dealt with by

---

[1] 1945 has only been chosen as a date of convenience. The already very great volume of judicial and arbitral development by that date is fully reviewed in such works as Ralston, *International Arbitration from Athens to Locarno* (1929), Hudson, *PCIJ*, Simpson and Fox, *International Arbitration* (1959) and Stuyt, *Survey of International Arbitrations 1794-1970* (1972). For more recent developments, see generally Tomuschat, "International Courts and Tribunals with Regionally Restricted and/or Specialized Jurisdiction", in Max Planck Institute for International Law, *Judicial Settlement of International Disputes* (1974), 285-416; Bernhardt (ed.), 1 *Encyclopedia of Public International Law, Settlement of Disputes (1981)*, *passim*; O-F & W; and Merrills, *International Dispute Settlement* (2nd ed., 1991).

specially constituted arbitration tribunals. In some instances the use of this procedure was prescribed by international agreements which pre-dated the existence of the ICJ; but in most of them the selection of arbitration in preference to recourse to the ICJ represented a deliberate choice of the former over the latter.

If we peruse the volumes of the *International Law Reports* (a series now of 83 volumes which, in passing, it should be mentioned that McNair and Lauterpacht founded just over 60 years ago)[2] we can find, working backwards over the past 45 years, that the following disputes, amongst others, have been referred to arbitration, evidently in preference to submission to the ICJ: a fisheries dispute between France and Canada;[3] land boundary disputes between Egypt and Israel,[4] Argentina and Chile[5] and India and Pakistan;[6] maritime boundary disputes between Guinea and Guinea-Bissau,[7] Iceland and Norway,[8] Argentina and Chile,[9] and between France and Britain;[10] a dispute relating to the destruction of the *Rainbow Warrior* between New Zealand and France;[11] the interpretation of two air service agreements between France and the United States[12] and one between Italy and the United States;[13] disputes between Portugal and Liberia[14] and between Ghana and Portugal[15] about

---

[2] The editing of this series continues at Cambridge University under the auspices of the Research Centre for International Law.
[3] *La Bretagne* (1986), 82 *ILR* 590.
[4] *Taba Award* (1988), 80 *ILR* 224.
[5] *Palena Case*, 38 *ILR* 10.
[6] *Rann of Kutch Case (India/Pakistan)*, 50 *ILR* 1.
[7] 77 *ILR* 635.
[8] *Jan Mayen Continental Shelf Delimitation*, 62 *ILR* 6.
[9] *Beagle Channel Case*, 52 *ILR* 93. Although this case took the form of an arbitration under the 1902 Arbitration Agreement between Argentina and Chile, in actual fact the arbitral tribunal consisted of five serving judges of the ICJ. This represented a compromise between Chile, which wished the case to be decided under the arbitration procedure previously agreed between the parties, and Argentina, which wished the case to be decided by the ICJ.
[10] *Anglo-French Continental Shelf Case*, 54 *ILR* 6.
[11] *The Rainbow Warrior*, 74 *ILR* 241 (ruling by the Secretary-General of the UN) and 82 *ILR* 499 (decision of the arbitral tribunal).
[12] 28 June 1964, 38 *ILR* 10; 9 December 1978, 54 *ILR* 303.
[13] 45 *ILR* 393.
[14] 36 *ILR* 351.
[15] 35 *ILR* 285.

THE INCREASE IN TRIBUNALS

the application of the ILO Abolition of Forced Labour Convention; a dispute concerning the use of the waters of Lac Lanoux between France and Spain;[16] a dispute relating to a denial of justice between Greece and the United Kingdom;[17] a dispute relating to the rate of exchange applicable to an intergovernmental financial agreement between Greece and the United Kingdom;[18] a dispute within UNESCO relating to eligibility for re-election to the Executive Board;[19] and a dispute relating to gold looted by Germany from Rome.[20]

Moreover, many treaties exist, and more are still being made,[21] which contain provisions for the compulsory settlement of disputes by special tribunals rather than by reference to the ICJ. During the period immediately following the end of the Second World War a number of tribunals were established to deal with claims arising out of the war – usually involving property rights of Allied nationals in former enemy territories: there was an Arbitral Commission for Property, Rights and Interests in Germany[22] as well as a Mixed Commission and a Tribunal on German External Debts.[23] In respect of Italy, bilateral tribunals called "Conciliation Commissions", but acting just like other international tribunals, were specially set up to deal with claims by United States,[24] French,[25] British,[26] Dutch[27] and Swiss[28] claims. Similarly, in the

---

[16] 24 *ILR* 101.
[17] 23 *ILR* 306.
[18] *In the Matter of the Diverted Cargoes* (1955), 22 *ILR* 820.
[19] 16 *ILR* 331.
[20] 20 *ILR* 441.
[21] See, generally, O-F & W.
[22] A number of the decisions of this tribunal are reported at various places in the *ILR* – see the volume containing the *Consolidated Table of Cases for Volumes 1-80*, 218-219.
[23] See, for Mixed Commission decisions, 25 *ILR* 326 and 35 *ILR* 253 and 261, and for Tribunal decisions, 25 *ILR* 33, 47 *ILR* 418 and 59 *ILR* 494.
[24] For cases, see under the name of the tribunal in volumes 22, 23, 24, 29, 30, 40 and 45 of the *ILR*.
[25] For cases, see under the name of the tribunal in volumes 18, 19, 20, 21, 22 and 25 of the *ILR*.
[26] For cases, see under the name of the tribunal in volumes 22 and 40 of the *ILR*.
[27] See 44 *ILR* 448.
[28] This was, in fact, a Permanent Conciliation Commission established under a treaty made in 1924. See 25 *ILR* 313.

case of Japan, commissions were established to deal with American,[29] British[30] and Dutch[31] claims.

In the same order of arrangements, though unconnected with post-war claims, is the Iran-US Claims Tribunal created in 1981 to resolve numerous disputes arising, principally, out of the treatment by Iran in the post-1979 period of contractual and property rights of American nationals in Iran. This tribunal has produced a body of decisions that has in nine years filled 23 volumes of its own series of reports.[32]

Thirdly, particular arrangements have been made for the settlement of specialized classes of dispute on a longer term basis. Amongst these are the arrangements relating to: commodity and trade disputes, such as those under the International Coffee Agreements[33] and GATT;[34] the law of the sea, including the Law of the Sea Tribunal,[35] arbitration procedures pertinent to oil pollution casualties[36] and prevention of marine pollution by dumping;[37] energy, including the European Nuclear Energy Tribunal[38] and the International Energy Agency Dispute Settlement Centre;[39] and air transport.[40]

Within this general category, perhaps the most important group of tribunals comprises those dealing with human rights. Beginning

---

[29] See 29 *ILR* 304, 307, 349, 414, 421, 431 and 438.
[30] See 29 *ILR* 40, 308, 318, 383, 389, 394 and 409.
[31] 30 *ILR* 520 and 525.
[32] *Iran-United States Claims Tribunal Reports*. See also various volumes of the *ILR* from volume 62 onwards.
[33] See *Report of the Advisory Panel on the Legality of a System for the Selective Adjustment of Quotas* (1965), 62 *ILR* 422 and *Findings of Arbitration Panel established under the Provisions of Art. 44*, 28 February 1969, 8 *ILM* 564 (1969). For the basic provisions, see O-F & W, 345-358.
[34] See, e.g., the arbitration between the United States and the EEC concerning poultry, which took the form of a request for an advisory opinion from a panel established by the GATT Council of Representatives, 21 Nov. 1963, 3 *ILM* 115 (1964).
[35] See below, pp. 19-22.
[36] International Convention Relating to Intervention on the High Seas in Cases of Oil Pollution Casualties, 1969, O-F & W, 569.
[37] Convention on the Prevention of Marine Pollution by Dumping of Wastes, 1972, O-F & W, 573.
[38] O-F & W, 518.
[39] Established on 23 July 1980.
[40] O-F & W, 487.

THE INCREASE IN TRIBUNALS

with the European Commission and the European Court of Human Rights operating under the European Convention on Human Rights of 1950, the system has been extended by the establishment in 1960 of the Inter-American Commission on Human Rights and in 1979 of the Inter-American Court of Human Rights and, since 1976, by the Human Rights Committee of the UN, acting pursuant to the Optional Protocol to the International Covenant on Civil and Political Rights.

Also falling within this broad category is the International Centre for the Settlement of Investment Disputes (commonly called "ICSID") set up in 1966 by a treaty concluded under the auspices of the World Bank to deal with investment disputes between any State party to the treaty and nationals of any other State party.

The busiest court of all, the Court of Justice of the European Communities, is, of course, in many respects a quite different type of tribunal from those so far considered in that its principal area of jurisdiction is over disputes arising out of the application of Community law within the territory of its members. At the same time, the Court effectively remains an international tribunal in dealing with disputes between the Member States or between the Member States and organs of the Community, or even between organs of the Comunity itself arising directly out of the Community treaties. Although the law applicable to such disputes is part of "Community law" in the large sense, there is a segment of Community law which is really international law in the traditional sense, in that it regulates relations between States or between States and an international institution on the basis of a treaty – albeit a unique and special one.[41]

---

[41] Mention should also be made of the Administrative Tribunals of various international organizations. These deal with complaints by staff members relating to non-observance by the organizations of the terms of their employment. The principal tribunals are those of the UN, the ILO and the World Bank. Though not, of course, inter-State tribunals, they are "international" in the sense that they operate outside the jurisdictional control of any State and apply a body of law that is independent of the law of any State. See, generally, Amerasinghe, *The Law of the International Civil Service* (1988).

B. REASONS FOR THE INCREASE

What are the reasons for this proliferation of tribunals? Why is it that States do not simply provide that any and every dispute between them that is to be decided by the judicial process should be referred to the ICJ?

1. *The historical element*

First, there is an historical element. In the evolution of the machinery of international justice, the ICJ appeared at a relatively late stage. The use of other means of third-party settlement had been an established feature for nearly a century and a half before the PCIJ, the predecessor of the ICJ, was brought into existence in 1920. The process of arbitration was carried forward, in the nineteenth century, from the arbitral commissions established under the Jay Treaty of 1794 through a series of British-American Claims Commissions, dealing with claims arising out of the War of Independence, the War of 1812 and the Civil War; by numerous bilateral arbitrations dealing with boundary disputes and territorial claims; by a string of *ad hoc* arbitrations on other matters, including claims arising out of the treatment of aliens; by a number of other commissions adjudicating groups of claims between the United States on the one hand and, on the other, respectively, Britain, Mexico, Peru, Spain, France and also between Britain on the one hand and, on the other, Peru, Venezuela, and so on. The catalogue of arbitrations compiled by the Dutch scholar, Stuyt,[42] lists some 350 arbitrations during the period from 1799 to 1922 – a list which accords only one entry to each claims commission, no matter how many individual decisions it may have recorded. The overall number of arbitral awards rendered by 1922 thus runs to several thousand. Lastly, at the end of the nineteenth century an attempt was made to institutionalize arbitration by the establishment of the Permanent Court of Arbitration.

---

[42] Stuyt, *Survey of International Arbitrations, 1794-1970* (1972).

So it can readily be seen that when the concept of true judicial settlement was introduced in the form of the PCIJ in 1920, judicial settlement – apart from the short-lived Central American Court of Justice[43] – was novel rather than normal. States were much more accustomed to un-institutionalized dispute settlement. Accordingly, whenever in the period following 1922 States resorted to arbitration it was really a reversion to a state of nature. Things would, of course, have been different if the proposals made in 1920 that the PCIJ should have compulsory jurisdiction,[44] and repeated in 1945 in relation to the ICJ,[45] had been adopted. In that case, both Courts would have had jurisdiction in any case submitted to them by a State; judicial settlement would have become standard and arbitration would have been the exception. But that did not come about and so it is not surprising that States did not entirely shed their earlier habits of recourse to special arrangements. Indeed, in the period following the end of the First World War there was a massive increase in arbitrations which took the form of the Mixed Arbitral Tribunals and of the various Mixed Claims Commissions arising out of the internal strife in Mexico.

2. *Functional considerations*

Apart from the historical considerations, there are a number of significant functional reasons why States have chosen other fora than the ICJ for the settlement of disputes. One is that if States were to submit all their justiciable disputes to the ICJ, that tribunal would be unable to cope with the burden of work.[46]

---

[43] This Court was established in 1907 and came to an end in 1917. It possessed the unusual feature of being granted jurisdiction in cases brought by individuals as well as by the States parties to its Statute. Of the ten cases that came before it, five were brought by individuals but in all these the plaintiff's claim was held to be inadmissible. Its best known decision was the one rendered in the *Gulf of Fonseca* case between El Salvador and Nicaragua. See, generally, Hudson, *PCIJ*, Ch. 3, 42-70.
[44] See Hudson, *PCIJ*, 190-193.
[45] See Rosenne, *ICJ*, vol. I, 364-367. See also Ch. III below.
[46] It cannot, of course, be assumed that States specifically take into account the workload of the ICJ when deciding whether to use that tribunal or to go to arbitration. No doubt, there are some cases in which the Parties do not mind if there is a long delay
(*Continued on p. 16*)

At the present time two special features characterize the procedure of the ICJ. One is that the Court normally sits in its full membership of 15 judges, with the addition of one or two *ad hoc* judges. This means that, because every judge is involved in every case, the number of cases that the Court can handle at a time is self-evidently less than if it were to sit in divisions and thus be capable of dealing with several cases simultaneously. The increasing use that is now being made of Chambers may go some way towards achieving a *de facto* establishment of divisions of the Court. But to approach the problem of dividing the work of the ICJ through the present occasional use of Chambers is unsystematic and haphazard. Those Chambers that have so far been used have not been pre-constituted and the membership of the Court has not been evenly spread over them. Some judges have been more favoured by the parties than have others. Moreover, because Chambers have been regarded as exceptional the claims of the full Court to the participation in its work of those judges sitting in a Chamber and, likewise, to the services of the Registry and the use of the courtroom, tend to override the claims of the particular case being heard in the Chamber. Furthermore, in relation to the rendering of Advisory Opinions, which forms a significant part of the Court's workload, there is sufficient doubt at present about the permissibility of using Chambers to make it unlikely that they will be used in this connection – that is, unless the Statute of the Court either is formally amended or is made the subject of some quasi-statutory modification by the UN General Assembly.[47] In short, the use of Chambers in their present form will not so spread the Court's workload as to eliminate the need for recourse to other instruments of litigation.

---

before the case is decided. On the other hand, there are many cases in which the speed with which the tribunal will dispose of the matter is a material consideration.

Clearly the factors of delay and expense in international litigation have weighed heavily in the decisions of many States, involved in disputes affecting a significant number of the nationals of one of them, to conclude global or lump-sum settlement arrangements which involve the party receiving the compensation in providing at its own expense a domestic commission for the adjudication of claims covered by the settlement.

[47] See below, Ch. V.

Closely linked with the difficulty stemming from the participation of 15 judges in each case is the delay inherent in the procedure followed by the Court in arriving at its collegiate or collective judgment.[48] This requires both the written and the oral participation of every judge – a process which is very time consuming and allows little distribution of the work-load amongst the judges.

Also prominent in the making of the choice between the ICJ and another tribunal is the nature of the composition of the Court. There is an observable, though undocumented, reluctance on the part of a number of States to submit a matter which directly affects them alone to the decision of judges most of whom have no connection with the region in which the dispute originates and some of whom one or the other side believes, rightly or wrongly, to be politically unsympathetic.[49]

Another factor related to composition that is sometimes brought into play is that of specialist knowledge. The argument is occasionally advanced that technical cases require technically qualified judges. By implication, the suggestion is made that the judges of the ICJ do not possess the necessary level of technical (i.e. non-legal) qualification. The validity – or at any rate the universal validity – of this proposition may be questioned. First, one must ask – how technical can an international issue be? Presumably the determination of a boundary line, whether on land or at sea, is not too technical, because many such cases have been decided by the ICJ. The same is true of cases involving the responsibility of States,

---

[48] The procedure is described in the Court's own "Resolution concerning the Internal Judicial Practice of the Court" adopted on 12 April 1976 (see ICJ, *Acts and Documents concerning the Organization of the Court, No. 4, The Charter of the United Nations, Statute and Rules of Court and other Documents* (1978), 165). For a discussion of the procedure, see Sir Robert Jennings, "The Collegiate Responsibility and Authority of the International Court of Justice", in Dinstein (ed.), *International Law at a Time of Perplexity* (1988), 343.
[49] This feeling may be accentuated by the perception that some Judges come from States in which the independence of the judiciary is exceptional and that those same States, as well as others, have never been prepared to litigate their own disputes in the Court. Perhaps, as a result of the profound political developments that have occurred over the past two years in a number of States that until recently were ideologically hostile to the Court, this feeling may change.

even for the conduct of nuclear tests. For example, no one has suggested that the members of the ICJ were not technically competent to decide the *Nuclear Tests Case* commenced against France in 1972.[50] Of course, cases can arise that make great intellectual demands upon the judges in the sense, for example, that they may require the assimilation of a mass of detailed evidence – as in the case brought by Nicaragua against the United States, where the dissenting opinion of Judge Schwebel particularly brings out the complexities involved in the serious and rigorous sifting of evidence.[51] But so to describe difficult cases that may confront the Court does not lead to the conclusion that the Court cannot handle them. It merely describes the task of the Court in some cases. Moreover, it should not be forgotten that the Court may call upon experts to assist it in its task – whether it is in valuing property, in assessing damage to warships, in applying technical cartographic concepts or in determining the significance of radioactive fallout.

All this said, however, the case for a specialist tribunal is strong where it is foreseen that there will be many cases with similar issues, to be decided over a relatively short time span, and in which the knowledge gained in deciding one will be of direct relevance in deciding others. For this reason, the weight of case numbers aside, it makes sense to assign to a claims commission a series of claims arising out of a given occurrence, such as the claims against Germany arising out of the First World War or the claims against Iran arising out of the events of 1979-1980. Similarly, in relation to the question of how the international judicial system can contribute to the evolution and application of international standards for the protection of the environment, it seems likely that the use of an expert tribunal will be helpful.

In principle, there can be no objection to the multiplication of

---

[50] *Nuclear Tests (Australia v. France) (Request for the Indication of Interim Measures of Protection)*, Order of 22 June 1973, *ICJ Reports 1973*, 99, 57 *ILR* 360; Judgment of 20 December 1974, *ICJ Reports 1974*, 253, 57 *ILR* 398.

[51] *Case concerning Military and Paramilitary Activities in and against Nicaragua (Nicaragua v. United States of America) (Merits)*, *ICJ Reports 1986*, 14, 76 *ILR* 349. The dissenting opinion of Judge Schwebel begins at *ICJ Reports 1986*, 259, 76 *ILR* 593.

international tribunals provided that there is sufficient work for them. It is only if an existing tribunal is capable of coping with the additional flow of work, and yet is not adopted for that purpose, that one needs to question the value of establishing the additional forum. A good illustration of what probably is an unnecessary duplication of arrangements is to be found in the prospective establishment of the Law of the Sea Tribunal under the 1982 Convention on the Law of the Sea. Part XV of this Convention contains an elaborate structure for the settlement of disputes which offers the parties a choice of recourse to a new Law of the Sea Tribunal, or to the ICJ, or to one kind of specially constituted arbitral tribunal for some purposes and to another arbitral tribunal for more limited purposes. Given the apparent reluctance of some States to commit themselves to the jurisdiction of the ICJ because its membership is geographically divorced from the region in which the case arises, one can understand the provision of arbitration as an alternative. But why should it be necessary to provide for a complete additional tribunal?

The political origin of the LOS Tribunal appears to lie in the initiative taken by the United States at a relatively early stage in the negotiations. This initiative reflected the firm belief of that country that the comprehensive regulation of so important an area of the law as that relating to the sea must be accompanied by effective judicial machinery for the settlement of disputes. Coupled with this was the concern felt at that time, because of the criticism of the ICJ, especially by developing countries in the UN General Assembly, following its judgment in the *South West Africa Cases*,[52] that that Court would not be acceptable as the exclusive forum for settling disputes arising under any new Convention. Once the idea of an additional tribunal had taken root, there appeared to be no inclination to question it.[53] But that does not mean that an institution conceived nearly a quarter of a century ago, but not yet born, must necessarily be allowed to reach term; and the

---

[52] *ICJ Reports 1966*, 3, 37 *ILR* 243
[53] See also Nordquist (ed.), *United Nations Convention on the Law of the Sea 1982, A Commentary*, vol. 5 (Rosenne and Sohn, vol. eds.) (1989), 6.

justification for it may properly be reviewed in the light of evolving circumstances.

Basically, the LOS Tribunal will not be very different from the ICJ – except that it will consist of 21 members (not 15 as in the ICJ) who are not expected to be full-time judges.[54] Its jurisdiction, which comprises all disputes submitted to it in accordance with the Convention, is therefore essentially concerned with traditional maritime matters of a kind which the ICJ is perfectly competent to handle and has repeatedly dealt with in the past. This is in a sense recognized by the fact that recourse to the ICJ is itself a permitted option under the Convention's dispute settlement system.

There is, however, one category of disputes that might arise under the Convention with which the ICJ is not able to deal under its Statute as framed at present, namely, that which involves the exercise of procedural rights directly by non-State entities, whether natural or legal persons. However, this prospect is quite narrow. It is limited to disputes that may arise under Articles 187 and 292 of the Convention. The first of these Articles foresees the reference to the Sea-Bed Disputes Chamber of the LOS Tribunal of a range of disputes arising in connection with the exploitation of the seabed beyond the limits of national jurisdiction and involving as parties not only States Parties to the Convention but also the Authority (an international organization), the Enterprise (likewise an international organization), State enterprises (which are, of course, not States) and national or juridical persons (which are likewise not States). In view of the provision in Article 34 of the Statute of the ICJ that "only States may be parties to disputes before the Court", it is clear that the ICJ would not be authorized

---

[54] Although the Convention does not state expressly that the members of the Tribunal will be part-time, this conclusion may be drawn from two provisions. First, Art. 7, dealing with incompatible activities, does not contain the prohibition of engaging in any other occupation of a professional nature that appears in the comparable article (Art. 16) of the Statute of the ICJ. Second, Art. 18, on the remuneration of members, describes it not in terms of "an annual salary" (as does Art. 32 of the Statute of the ICJ) but in terms of "an annual allowance and, for each day on which he exercises his functions, a special allowance". The same view is expressed in the Commentary, 351.

REASONS FOR THE INCREASE 21

to deal with these cases. Nor would the ICJ be permitted to deal with a case arising under Article 292 of the Convention, on the prompt release of vessels, if the parties (of which one would in this situation be a non-State entity) were to agree to submit the case to an international tribunal.

Do these two extensions of the competence of the LOS Tribunal to cases involving non-State parties warrant the construction of a whole additional judicial system to deal with LOS Convention problems – especially when the new Tribunal is not given an exclusive jurisdiction over such questions? That question appears to have occasioned little, if any, specific discussion in the LOS Conference. Now that one can, admittedly with the benefit of hindsight, review the situation with more detachment and see how transient was the impact of the *South West Africa* judgment, one may well wonder whether some of the effort that went into constructing a tribunal that so closely parallels the ICJ could not have been better employed in determining how the Statute of the ICJ itself might have been revised to enable that body to deal with these additional categories of cases. It is sometimes difficult to reject the thought that a number of States – once the proposal for a new tribunal had been launched by the United States – accorded an undeclared priority to creating twenty-one more judicial posts in the world. If this is the reason for the establishment of the new LOS Tribunal, it is not a sufficient one.

The international community would do well to consider whether, even at this late stage, and within the framework of the Decade of International Law that is to run from now to 2000, there would not be advantage in amending the Statute of the ICJ so as also to permit access to the Court in the limited class of cases that seems to be the only advance that the LOS Tribunal has to offer over the ICJ. If such amendments to the Statute of the ICJ were to be made, the Law of the Sea Treaty could at the same time – perhaps even as part of the same process[55] – be amended to delete

---

[55] This is not to suggest that a *single* instrument could achieve this dual objective. The amendment to the Statute of the ICJ would have to be carried out by one instrument to
(*Continued on p. 22*)

the provisions for the establishment and operation of the LOS Tribunal. The justification for such a development would not lie simply in the considerable financial savings that would be achieved (though they should not be lightly dismissed), nor in the elimination of a risk of diversity of approach and substantive decision between two major international tribunals. The real justification would lie in the simple good sense of not doing something unnecessary.

satisfy the requirements of Art. 69 of the Statute and Art. 108 of the Charter; the amendment to the Law of the Sea Convention would have to be carried out by another. As the Convention has not yet entered into force, it would not seem essential to follow the amendment procedures prescribed in Arts. 312 and 313 of the Convention. Given that the signatories of the LOS Convention are virtually identical with membership of the UN, there would not appear to be any insuperable difficulty in combining the procedures leading to the adoption, signature and eventual ratification of the two instruments.

CHAPTER III

CONSENT

A. CONSENT GENERALLY

As things stand at present the system of international adjudication is totally dependent upon the consent of the parties. The ICJ has no jurisdiction unless the parties have specifically agreed thereto either through a treaty or by accepting the Optional Clause in appropriate terms. Every other tribunal, whether specially created or institutional, is likewise dependent upon the consent of the parties. It hardly needs to be said how basic this assumption is. The requirement is normally rigorously applied and is reflected in practice by, for example, the presumption in favour of the State against which jurisdiction is being invoked.

Yet some cracks in the edifice are developing, though, it would seem, less from any critical approach to the concept of consent than from the seeming disinclination of the Court to forego jurisdiction in certain cases in which there is at any rate an arguable case that consent has been given. Thus, in the case concerning *Military and Paramilitary Activities in and against Nicaragua, Jurisdiction and Admissibility*[1] the Court by a majority, and in the face of very strongly argued dissent, held that an unratified declaration by Nicaragua under Article 36(2) of the Statute of the PCIJ was capable of founding the jurisdiction of the ICJ under Article 36(5) of its Statute. The same predisposition to find a source of consent reappears in the Court's subsequent judgment in the case brought by Nicaragua against Honduras in respect of *Border and Transborder Armed Actions*[2] – notwithstanding the Court's repetition of the traditional formula that it would "have to consider whether

---

[1] *Nicaragua v. USA, ICJ Reports 1984*, 392, 76 *ILR* 104.
[2] *Jurisdiction and Admissibility, ICJ Reports 1988*, 69.

the force of the arguments militating in favour of jurisdiction is preponderant, and to 'ascertain whether an intention on the part of the Parties exists to confer jurisdiction upon it'".[3]

While obviously we must welcome any evidence of a growing willingness on the part of tribunals to find, and of States to accept, grounds for the exercise of compulsory jurisdiction, the fact remains that a significant division is emerging between theory and practice in relation to the compulsory exercise of international jurisdiction of which States and scholars appear as yet to have taken relatively little notice. This development fundamentally affects the validity of the general assumption that specific consent is necessary for the exercise of international jurisdiction.

There appear to be two reasons for the requirement of specific consent: one formal; the other substantial. The formal one really amounts to no more than a repetition of the requirement itself – a State is not subject to jurisdiction without its consent because it is not so subject; or because to be so subject might be inconsistent with such doctrines as the dignity and equality of States. These reasons have only to be stated for their formal or nominal quality to be evident. But what is the substantial or, more to the point, the functional reason why such specific consent is necessary? To reply that in the absence of consent a State might be taken to court by an unwelcome plaintiff is not a sufficient answer. Nor is it an adequate answer to say that matters about which States may be sued are so important or vital that express consent is an essential precondition of litigation. There is nothing so inherently special about States that when it comes to a fundamental aspect of the legal system – namely, exposure to judicial redress – they should not be treated in the same way as individuals. The "functional" argument, it would seem, eventually turns out to be a "formal" one.[4] Nor again is it

---

[3] *Ibid.* at 76.

[4] The same kind of analysis can be applied to the immunity enjoyed by States from the exercise of jurisdiction over them by the Courts of foreign States. The erosion of State immunity in domestic fora reflects a general awareness of the lack of justification for any comprehensive immunity of States. Whether the retention of immunity in cases *jure imperii* or not involving commercial transactions still reflects any real need of States will be considered below, this Chapter, Section E.

enough to assert that consent is required because it always has been required and that that is the way States want it. It is the very validity of this assertion that falls to be questioned.

The rest of this chapter will be devoted to an examination of three situations which suggest that both on the judicial plane and, even more important, in State practice, the requirement for exact consent, closely linked in time and substance to the exercise of jurisdiction, may have become so worn away as to require a profound reconsideration of the fundamentals of the subject. Each of these situations involves an exercise of jurisdiction of a judicial or quasi-judicial character – one by the ICJ, the second by the Inter-American Commission on Human Rights (the IACHR) and the third by the Security Council of the UN. Though it is possible to trace the exercise of jurisdiction in each instance to some act of consent, it is to be observed that in each case that act is so remote from the occasion on which it became relevant as to suggest the questions: if this is consent, is consent really necessary; what significant political function does it serve; is not the self-presentation by a State as a member of the international community and, in particular, as a Member of the United Nations, a sufficient consent to participation in community processes to warrant the exercise of the judicial power, as one major function of international government, without the need for further consent?

The question of whether it is desirable for States to accept the compulsory jurisdiction of judicial organs is not a new one. It was discussed in such important contexts as the elaboration of the Statute of the PCIJ in 1920 and of the ICJ in 1945. But it was always discussed in terms of subjective preferences, not by reference to what was actually happening in the world. Now, however, evidence is accumulating that it is not correct to assume that jurisdiction is only exercised where there is clear consent.

Three leading examples of this evidence will now be considered. After that it will be possible to suggest some conclusions.

B. REJECTION BY THE INTERNATIONAL COURT OF JUSTICE OF THE NEED FOR A JURISDICTIONAL LINK IN INTERVENTION PROCEEDINGS

The first of these examples of relaxation of the requirement of consent is provided by the decision of a Chamber of the ICJ in the application by Nicaragua to intervene in the case brought before the Court by a special agreement concluded between El Salvador and Honduras.[5] Here the Chamber (which, admittedly, is not the same thing as the plenary Court, though for the purposes of the case the Chamber represents the Court[6]) resolved in a positive sense the previously controversial question of whether intervention may be permitted in a case in which there exists no specific jurisdictional link between the applicant State and the original Parties. In order to appreciate the significance of the episode it is necessary briefly to recall the recent history of applications to intervene in proceedings before the Court.

Article 62(1) of the Statute of the ICJ provides that "should a State consider that it has an interest of a legal nature which may be affected by the decision in the case, it may submit a request to the Court to be permitted to intervene". The Article contains no reference to the question of whether or not any jurisdictional link is required between the applicant State and the States already parties to the case.[7]

The question was first raised *obiter* in connection with the application by Fiji to intervene in the *Nuclear Tests* case between Australia and France.[8] When the Court held that the principal case no longer had an object,[9] it also determined in a separate Order[10]

---

[5] *Land, Island and Maritime Frontier Dispute (El Salvador/Honduras), Application to Intervene, Judgment, ICJ Reports 1990*, 92.
[6] See below, Ch. V, Section B.
[7] But in 1978 the Court introduced, as Art. 81(2)(c) of the revised Rules of the Court, a requirement that a State applying to intervene must specify "any basis of jurisdiction which is claimed to exist as between the State applying to intervene and the parties to the case".
[8] *ICJ Reports 1974*, 253, 57 *ILR* 398.
[9] By reason of the unilateral declarations made by France to the effect that it would discontinue atmospheric nuclear testing.
[10] *ICJ Reports 1974*, 535, 57 *ILR* 601.

that the application of Fiji to intervene had in consequence lapsed. Judge Onyeama appended a declaration stating that the application should have been rejected on the ground that there was no jurisdictional link between Fiji and France.[11] Judges Dillard and Sir Humphrey Waldock made a joint declaration to the effect that, if the main case had proceeded, it would have been necessary to examine whether or not there existed between Fiji and France a sufficient jurisdictional link to support Fiji's application under Art. 62.[12] Judge Jiménez de Aréchaga went further. He stated that "for the purpose of asserting a right as against the respondent a State must be in a position in which it could itself bring the respondent before the Court".[13] His reasoning started from the consideration that, at the time Article 62 was first drafted as part of the Statute of the PCIJ, it was assumed that that Court would possess general compulsory jurisdiction and that therefore nothing need be said about a jurisdictional requirement in the context of intervention. He then observed that the provision for general compulsory jurisdiction had not survived and that as a result Article 62 must be interpreted and applied as subject to the conditions laid down in the optional clause: "Otherwise, unreasonable consequences would result, in conflict with basic principles such as those of equality of parties before the Court and the strict reciprocity of rights and obligations among the States which accept its jurisdiction".[14]

In subsequent cases in which applications to intervene were made, those by Malta in the *Tunisia/Libya Continental Shelf* case[15] and by Italy in the *Libya/Malta Continental Shelf* case,[16] the Court did not need to deal with this question because it found in each case that there were other grounds for rejecting the application to intervene. However, in the Nicaraguan application to intervene in

---

[11] *ICJ Reports 1974*, 531, 57 *ILR* 602.
[12] *ICJ Reports 1974*, 532, 57 *ILR* 603.
[13] *Id.*
[14] *Id.* This reasoning was amplified in the same Judge's Separate Opinion in Italy's application to intervene in the *Libya/Malta* case, *ICJ Reports 1984*, 55, esp. 66-68, 70 *ILR* 527, esp. 595-597.
[15] *ICJ Reports 1981*, 3, 62 *ILR* 608.
[16] *ICJ Reports 1989*, 3, 70 *ILR* 527.

the *El Salvador/Honduras*[17] case, the Chamber found that Nicaragua had a legal interest in the case that might be affected by the decision and, accordingly, that in principle Nicaragua might intervene. The question of the need for a jurisdictional link therefore had to be resolved.

The Chamber's treatment of the matter is remarkable for its brevity. The essentials of its reasoning are contained in one sentence: "The competence of the Court in this matter of intervention is not, like its competence to hear and determine the dispute referred to it, derived from the consent of the parties to the case, but from the consent given by them, in becoming parties to the Court's Statute, to the Court's exercise of its powers conferred by the Statute".[18] This statement is all the more striking when it is read against the background not only of the earlier debate on the issue and, in particular, the detailed argument developed by Judge Jiménez de Aréchaga on the basis of the *travaux préparatoires* of the Statute of the PCIJ, but also of the Chamber's own acknowledgment of "the general principle of consensual jurisdiction".

The extent to which this decision can be taken as a precursor of a more "relaxed" approach within the Court to problems of jurisdiction and consent cannot be predicted. It must be remembered that each of the three titular judges in the Chamber had previously, when sitting as members of the full Court, expressed doubts about the need for a jurisdictional link. Judge Oda, in his separate opinion on the application by Malta to intervene in the *Tunisia/Libya* case, had said: "if the third State does not have a proper jurisdictional link with the original litigant States, it can nevertheless participate, but not as a party within the meaning of the term in municipal law".[19] Judge Sette-Camara in his dissenting opinion on the Italian application to intervene in the *Libya/Malta* case had expressed himself more broadly, attributing his conclusion that a jurisdictional link was not necessary to the fact that intervention is an incidental procedure grafted onto the main case. "The Court will entertain this preliminary procedure within

---

[17] *ICJ Reports 1990*, 92.
[18] *Ibid.*, 133, para. 96.
[19] *ICJ Reports 1981*, at 27, 62 *ILR*, at 636.

the framework of the principal case, jurisdiction being established by the main litigants."[20] The Judge did not distinguish between an application to intervene as a party and an application to intervene as a non-party. Judge Jennings had in the same case also expressed a view that because of the limited nature of the Italian application, there was no need for a jurisdictional link.[21]

It is, therefore, possible that in future cases a distinction may be drawn between the case in which the applicant State is allowed to intervene other than as a party (in which case a jurisdictional link is not required) and the case in which the applicant State is allowed to become a party (in which case a jurisdictional link *may* be required) – "*may*" because Article 62 does not distinguish between the two situations and it would be strange if it required a jurisdictional link in one and not in the other of the two situations. But, though the position is not entirely clear, the fact remains that a Chamber of the Court has dealt with the question of jurisdiction in a manner that appears to differ from the way in which the full Court has dealt with comparable problems in the past. If a Chamber does not feel itself bound by the views expressed by the full Court, presumably the full Court will not feel itself bound by the views of the Chamber. This does not mean, however, that in the future the full Court must adhere to the position it has adopted in the past. Of the fourteen titular judges that sat in the last of the intervention cases prior to the Nicaraguan application, only seven remain on the Court and, of those, three have already clearly pronounced themselves against the need for a jurisdictional link and one has done so by implication – at any rate in cases where the applicant State seeks to intervene other than as a party.[22] The possibility is thus by no means excluded that the full Court, now with a markedly different composition, may yet adopt a view on the

---

[20] *ICJ Reports 1984*, at 86, 70 *ILR*, at 615.
[21] *ICJ Reports 1984*, at 155-156, 70 *ILR*, at 684-685.
[22] Judge Schwebel dealt with the question in his dissenting opinion on the Italian application to intervene in the *Libya/Malta* case. (*ICJ Reports 1984*, at 139-147, 70 *ILR* 668-676.) Judge Ago, though dissenting and favouring acceptance of the Italian application, did not deal expressly with the question. By implication, however, he must have considered the absence of a jurisdictional link as irrelevant; otherwise, he could not have reached his main conclusion. (*ICJ Reports 1984*, 115, 70 *ILR* 644.)

jurisdictional aspect of intervention more favourable to the State seeking to intervene. What cannot be gainsaid, however, is that in terms of the Court's approach to the requirement of consent for participation in contentious proceedings, the practical consequence of the decision on the Nicaraguan application is a significant relaxation in the severity of the Court's requirement of consent. The words actually used may sometimes suggest the contrary, but what matters most is the substantive conclusion. And what matters also is that the States that were the original parties to the case have not contested the Chamber's conclusion.

C. THE EXTENSION OF JURISDICTION OF THE INTER-AMERICAN COMMISSION ON HUMAN RIGHTS

It is, of course, possible to seek to diminish the significance of the development just cited by suggesting that it is largely technical and does not really affect the States concerned in any politically significant sensitive spot. Even if this were true – and it is strongly arguable that the last point is not – the situation to which we now turn is of an entirely different order. Here we shall be dealing with an expansion of jurisdiction in the delicate area of compliance with human rights. This illustration of the relaxation of the standards of consent required to support an exercise of international jurisdiction is provided by the manner in which the Inter-American Commission on Human Rights (IACHR) has conducted itself in relation to petitions filed against those Members of the Organization of American States (OAS) that are not parties to the American Convention on Human Rights (the American Convention). At the present time they are Chile, Cuba, Paraguay and the United States. The Convention is the only legally binding treaty on human rights operating in the Inter-American system and the Commission has quite rightly treated non-parties as not directly bound by it. The Commission has nonetheless applied to those non-parties the human rights standards that are prescribed in the American Declaration of the Rights and Duties of Men (the American Declaration). The normative quality of this instrument has been derived by the Commission from the fact that it was adopted as a resolution by the General Council of the OAS, of which Chile, Cuba, Paraguay and the United States are members. Its application to these States[23] and particularly the United States, warrants some further description.

In many quarters the belief has long prevailed that the United States is not subject to any binding obligations in respect of international human rights standards in respect of which international compliance procedures can be invoked against it. In fact, the reverse is true, as is shown by a number of resolutions or other instruments containing the specific conclusions of the IACHR on individual petitions alleging failures of the United States to comply with the human rights standards laid down in the American Declaration. This relatively small, but highly significant, jurisprudence deserves to be much better known than it seems to be.[24]

---

[23] There have also been a number of cases arising out of events in Chile, Cuba and Paraguay. See, for example:
- Chile: IACHR, *Annual Report, 1984-1985*, 34-50;
- Cuba: IACHR, *Annual Report, 1980-1981*, 87-103;
- Paraguay: IACHR, *Annual Report, 1986-1987*, 111.

Although the substance of these cases is not described here, they give rise to the same jurisdictional issues as are posed by the cases against the United States – but with the possible qualification that these other countries may have done less in the way of conduct amounting to acquiescence in the extension of the jurisdiction of the Commission.

[24] The primary materials are to be found in the following documents of the Organization of American States:
– *Basic Documents Pertaining to Human Rights in the Inter-American System (updated to 1 March 1988)*, OEA/Ser. L.V/II.71, Doc. 6 rev. 1;
– various *Annual Reports* of the IACHR, especially those for 1980-1981, 1986-1987, 1988-1989 and 1989-1990. These *Reports*, though containing a comprehensive survey of the activities of the Commission for the years in question, each have a section devoted specifically to the action of the Commission in relation to petitions filed with it. This part of the *Report* consists of a series of decisions comparable to those of the European Commission on Human Rights or the UN Committee on Human Rights.

The literature on this particular aspect of the Inter-American human rights system is surprisingly sparse – notably in the leading American international law periodicals. Of the various petitions affecting the United States dealt with by the IACHR, only two appear to have been noted in the *AJIL*. See Fox, "Inter-American Commission on Human Rights finds United States in Violation", 82 *AJIL* 600 (1988). None of the decisions has appeared in *ILM*. Only one reference to the procedure appears in *DUSPIL*, in the volume for 1980, at 243-252. While Professor T. Buergenthal in his
(*Continued on p. 32*)

There appear[25] to have been four cases involving the United States. The first,[26] filed in 1977 and concluded in 1981, asserted that an abortion carried out in a Boston hospital was a violation of the right to life granted by the American Declaration. The United States did not deny either the applicability of the Declaration or the permissibility of filing the petition or the competence of the Commission. The Commission considered the substance of the complaint and concluded by four votes to three that the facts did not constitute a violation of the American Declaration.

The second case dealt with two petitions filed on behalf of two young men under the age of 18 who had already been executed, one in South Carolina, the other in Texas, for rape and murder.[27] It was alleged that the provisions of the American Declaration protecting the right to life and the special rights of children and prohibiting cruel, infamous or unusual punishments had been violated. The Commission concluded by five votes to one in both cases that the United States Government had violated Article I (right to life) and Article II (right to equality before the law) in respect of the two petitioners. Again, the United States Government participated in the case without challenge to the right of the Commission to deal with it.[28] After the adoption of the

---

important contributions to the subject mentions the availability of the procedures in general terms, he does not specifically identify their applicability to the United States. See, e.g., his article "The Revised OAS Charter and the Protection of Human Rights", 69 *AJIL* 828 (1975) and his report on "Implementation in the Inter-American Human Rights System" in Bernhardt and Jolowicz (eds.), *International Enforcement of Human Rights* (1985), 57.

[25] One is obliged to use the word "appear" because it is difficult to be certain on perusal of the relevant sources that one has found them all. For example, the item mentioned in *DUSPIL* (see n. 24 above) cannot be traced in the *Annual Reports* of the IACHR.

[26] *White and Potter*. Petitions filed 19 Jan. 1977. Decided on 6 March 1981, by Resolution No. 23/81. IACHR, *Annual Report, 1980-1981*, 25.

[27] *Roach and Pinkerton*. Petitions filed on 4 December 1985 and 8 May 1986. Case 9647. Decided on 27 March 1987 by Resolution No. 3/87. Reported in IACHR, *Annual Report 1986-1987*, 147.

[28] In dealing with the substantive human rights issues the arguments in the case discussed major questions of international law of wide significance such as the formation of customary international law, particularly the effect of protest against an evolving norm and the concept of *jus cogens*.

Resolution, the United States requested "reconsideration", which was granted, but the Commission decided, by a majority vote, not to modify its decision.[29]

The third decision concerned a petition filed on behalf of "unnamed, unnumbered residents, both living and dead", of an insane asylum in Grenada that was bombed by United States military aircraft during the intervention in that country in 1983.[30] The applicants alleged violations of Articles I and II of the American Declaration and of the Fourth Geneva Convention Relative to the Protection of Civilian Persons in Time of War. Subsequently, after the United States sought to have the petition declared inadmissible, the petitioners were identified by name. The application was declared admissible. Once more, the United States Government participated. The substantive outcome is not yet reported.

The fourth case dealt with a petition filed on behalf of, in the words of the decision, "an impoverished young black" who was executed for the rape and murder of an elderly white woman.[31] The petition claimed violations of Article I (right to life), Article II (equality before the law) and Article XXVI (right to due process of law). The petition was declared inadmissible for failure to state facts constituting a violation of the rights set forth in the American Declaration. The United States Government participated in the proceedings.

While it would be interesting to go further into these cases, it must be recalled that our focus in the present discussion is not upon their substance but upon their relevance to the broader question of the nature and form of the consent that is required of States if they are to endow international bodies with jurisdiction to review their conduct under international law. In particular, in

---

[29] *Ibid.*, 184.
[30] Application No. 9213 by *Disabled Peoples International et al.* Complaint filed on 5 November 1983. Admissibility upheld. Reported in IACHR, *Annual Report, 1986-1987*, 184.
[31] *Constantine*. Case No. 23/89. Petition filed 15 July 1987. Decided on 28 September 1989. Reported in IACHR, *Annual Report 1989-1990*, 62.

34   CONSENT

what way did the United States give its consent to the exercise by the IACHR of jurisdiction in these cases?

In reviewing the pertinent texts, the natural starting point is the Statute of the very body that has exercised the jurisdiction in question, namely, the IACHR.[32] Chapter IV, entitled "Functions and Powers", distinguishes expressly between the powers possessed by the Commission with respect to those States that are Parties to the American Convention and those that are not. As regards the latter, Article 20(b) empowers the Commission to examine communications submitted to it and any other available information, to address the government of any Member State not a Party to the Convention for information deemed pertinent by the Commission, and to make recommendations to such State, when it finds it appropriate, in order to bring about more effective observance of fundamental human rights.

Since the legal effectiveness of this grant of powers in relation to non-Parties to the American Convention is not directly supported by any treaty text, in contrast with the position in relation to States that are Parties to that Convention,[33] one must next ask what is the legal character and position of the Statute. Despite the frequent association between the word "Statute" and the idea of a treaty, there is no legal requirement that every statute must be a treaty; and the Statute of the Commission is not one. It is described as having been "Approved by Resolution No. 447 taken by the General Assembly of the OAS at its Ninth Regular Session, held in La Paz, Bolivia, October 1979".

This Resolution,[34] in its turn, declared in its recitals "that pursuant to Article 52 of the Charter, the General Assembly has

---

[32] See *Basic Documents*, 65.
[33] The position of the IACHR is expressly regulated by Chapter VII of the American Convention. In particular, Art. 41(f) empowers it to take action on petitions under the provisions of Arts. 44 and 51 of the American Convention. These deal with the competence of the Commission, including the requirement of the exhaustion of local remedies, and procedure. Therefore, so far as States Parties to the Convention are concerned there is a clear and short jurisdictional link to the Commission.
[34] Text in OAS, *Inter-American Commission on Human Rights, Ten Years of Activities, 1971-1981* (1982), 387.

the power to determine the structure and functions of the Organs of the Organization". In its operative part the Resolution approved the Statute of the Commission contained in the Resolution. We then have to move back to Article 52 of the Charter[35] to find that "the General Assembly is the supreme organ" of the OAS and that it has the power, amongst others, "(a) to decide the general action and policy of the Organization, *determine the structure and functions of its organs*, and consider any matter relating to friendly relations among the American States".[36] It thus appears from the italicized words that the General Assembly possessed and exercised the power to create the IACHR as an organ; and this result is expressly reflected in Article 1(1) of the Statute in these words:

> The Inter-American Commission on Human Rights is an organ of the Organization of the American States, created to promote the observance and defence of human rights and to serve as consultative organ of the Organization in this matter.

At this point the linkage of the exercise of the powers of the IACHR to a specific treaty undertaking is complete.[37] But the

---

[35] This is not the original Charter as adopted at Bogotá in 1948 but the Charter as amended by a Protocol of Amendment, known as the "Protocol of Buenos Aires", signed on 27 February 1967. Text in 6 *ILM* 310 (1967). This replaced the whole of the original Chapter X entitled "The Inter-American Conference" by a new Chapter XI entitled "The General Assembly" (*ibid.*, 325). The Protocol was ratified by the United States after the President had obtained the advice and consent of the Senate.

[36] Emphasis supplied.

[37] This analysis may be compared with the manner in which the IACHR itself set out the basis of its action in relation to the United States in *White and Potter*, Resolution No. 23/81, of 6 March 1981, IACHR, *Annual Report, 1980-1981*, 25 at 38-39:
"15. The international obligation of the United States of America, as a member of the Organization of American States (OAS), under the jurisdiction of the Inter-American Commission on Human Rights (IACHR) is governed by the Charter of OAS (Bogotá, 1948) as amended by the Protocol of Buenos Aires on February 27, 1967, ratified by United States on April 23, 1968.
16. As a consequence of articles 3*j*, 16, 51 *e*, 112 and 150 of this Treaty, the provisions of
(*Continued on p. 36*)

point to be noted is the distant or slender character of the connection. When the United States Senate advised and consented to the ratification of the Protocol of Buenos Aires in 1967 it seems unlikely that it foresaw that it was thereby impliedly giving its consent to the eventual exercise of jurisdiction over matters otherwise falling within the domestic jurisdiction of the United States by a Commission empowered to apply to the United States standards not even prescribed in a binding treaty text.

In other words, the United States Government has not been an unwilling participant in the process of gradually developing the capacity of the IACHR to receive petitions alleging violations by the United States of the standards prescribed in the Inter-American Declaration. Indeed, in 1977, the then Secretary of State, Mr Vance, endorsed the role of the IACHR "as an independent monitor of human rights in the Americas" and went on to accord to the Commission, with immediate effect, the facility of carrying out "at times and places of its choosing" on-site investigations in the United States.[38]

In concluding this section, the point to be made is not so much that petitions against the United States and other non-parties to the American Convention have been dealt with by the IACHR as that the chain of consent leading to the exercise of jurisdiction by the Commission is so tenuous. This is not to suggest that there is anything wrong in the development. Quite the contrary. The extension of the competence of the IACHR is greatly to be

---

other instruments and resolutions of the OAS on human rights, acquired binding force. Those instruments and resolutions approved with the vote of U.S. Government, are the following:
– American Declaration of the Rights and Duties of Man (Bogotá, 1948)
– Statute and Regulations of the IACHR 1960, as amended by resolution XXII of the Second Special Inter-American Conference (Rio de Janeiro, 1965)
– Statute and Regulations of IACHR of 1979-1980.
  17. Both Statutes provide that, for the purpose of such instruments, the IACHR is the organ of the OAS entrusted with the competence to promote the observance and respect of human rights. For the purpose of the Statutes, human rights are understood to be the rights set forth in the American Declaration in relation to States not parties to the American Convention on Human Rights (San José, 1969). (Arts. 1 and 2 of 1960 Statute and Art. 1 of 1979 Statute.)"
[38] See *DUSPIL 1980*, 251.

welcomed. But what is important is that evidence of that consent is so piecemeal that its existence hardly seems to have secured public recognition. In such circumstances, one may well suggest that in practice the "principle of consent" in, at any rate, the field of human rights, is not really so important to the Inter-American community as traditional utterances by States and writers might otherwise appear to indicate.

D. THE QUASI-JUDICIAL ACTIVITY OF THE SECURITY COUNCIL

A further – even more significant – illustration of the same phenomenon is to be found in that most sensitive of all areas of State concern, international security. Here, too, States have acquiesced in the assumption by some international organs of an extraordinary degree of compulsory jurisdiction.[39] This takes the form principally of the manner in which the Security Council has exercised the quasi-judicial competence which it has arrogated to itself in the discharge of its undoubted duty to take decisions relating to threats to the peace, breaches of the peace and acts of aggression.[40] To appreciate why a procedure that originally appeared to be relevant only to the maintenance and restoration of international peace and security is also relevant here, where we are concerned with the administration of international justice, requires some introductory exposition.

As will be recalled, the summary description of the organs of the administration of international justice with which we began was limited to procedures traditionally recognized as judicial – the activities of international courts and arbitral tribunals expressly so called. In identifying the class of organs of present concern, reference was made to the traditional tripartite classification

---

[39] As will be explained later, even the Permanent Members of the Security Council, against whom no action can be taken without their consent, are parties to the development. While they are not the "victims" of the extension of Security Council jurisdiction, they have participated in it and, therefore, they are bound by their conduct and its implications.

[40] See the UN Charter, Chapters VI and VII.

familiar to the domestic lawyer and it was said that the present discussion relates only to the judicial aspect of the three divisions. At the same time, caution is called for in applying this classification to the international scene. The formal organization of the international community now includes a feature for which there is no clear parallel in the domestic scene – but it is nonetheless a phenomenon that touches closely upon our present subject. Its principal illustration is to be found in certain aspects of the activities of the General Assembly and the Security Council of the UN. For convenience we shall focus more closely upon the latter organ,[41] for it alone has decision-making authority binding upon States in the security sphere.

The Security Council, one must recall, is the body upon which the Charter places the primary responsibility for the maintenance

[41] The activity of the General Assembly as a political organ of the UN acting also in a quasi-judicial capacity was identified and accepted by the ICJ in the course of its advisory opinion on *Namibia* in 1971. (*Legal Consequences for States of the Continued Presence of South Africa in Namibia, ICJ Reports 1971*, 16, at 49, paras. 102-103, 49 *ILR*, at 39.) South Africa had argued that the General Assembly resolution of 1966 bringing the Mandate for South West Africa to an end was outside the powers of the General Assembly since it was not a judicial organ. The Court said:

"102. ...To deny a political organ of the United Nations ... the right to act, on the argument that it lacks the competence to render what is described as a judicial decision, would not only be inconsistent but would amount to a complete denial of the remedies available against fundamental breaches of an international undertaking.

103. The Court is unable to appreciate [sic] the view that the General Assembly acted unilaterally as party and judge in its own cause ... [T]he United Nations as a successor to the League acting through its competent organs, must be seen above all as the supervisory institution competent to pronounce, in that capacity, on the conduct of the mandatory with respect to its international obligations, and competent to act accordingly." [It appears that the word "appreciate" at the beginning of this sentence may be a typographical error and that the word should be "accept". Although the English text of the Advisory Opinion is authoritative, the French translation reads thus; "La Cour ne peut souscrire à l'opinion ..." – a translation that reflects the English verb "accept" rather than the verb "appreciate".]

Although the Court is not here expressly using the term "quasi-judicial", there is little room for doubt that in identifying the General Assembly as a "supervisory institution" it was according to that body the characteristics of a quasi-judicial body. It is difficult to conceive of a supervisory body that would not be bound to act, at the very least, in accordance with the rules of natural justice and, for that reason, be regarded as a quasi-judicial body.

Note should be taken of the views expressed by Judge Sir Gerald Fitzmaurice in Annex 1 to his Dissenting Opinion on "Incompetence of the UN Assembly to act as a court of law". (*ICJ Reports 1971*, 299; 49 *ILR* 288) and of Judge Gros, especially at *ICJ Reports 1971*, 340, para. 34, 49 *ILR* 330, para. 34.

of international peace and security. It has been given the power to identify the existence of threats to the peace, breaches of the peace and acts of aggression, as well as to determine what measures should be taken by States to restore international peace. It can thus easily be seen that there is no organ within any domestic legal framework that parallels this international instrument of collective peace-keeping. Certainly no legislature performs such a task; nor does any judiciary. To some extent it can be argued that the executive – and in particular any department of the executive charged with the preservation of public order – has a comparable dual function of identifying a breach of the law and then reacting to it. But, as is well known, such reaction is not, or is not meant to be, predominantly influenced by political considerations. Moreover, it is subject to judicial control – or is so, at any rate, within democratic societies. On the international scene it is quite different. The Security Council is not subject to any judicial control that can be invoked at the instance of a party against which it directs its political reaction. In itself, this should not be surprising. The circumstances in which the Security Council is called upon to act – threats to peace, breaches of the peace and acts of aggression – are ones which require an immediate and effective community response, whether by way of non-forcible measures, such as condemnation, or by calling upon the State concerned to desist from its action and restore the previous situation, or by stronger measures such as the interruption of economic relations, the imposition of blockade or even ultimately the collective use of force to terminate the abnormal situation.

There is, however, a feature of this collective response which, in considering the administration of justice in the international community with deliberate focus upon the judicial aspect, we cannot properly ignore. There have been a number of occasions on which, as part of its treatment of a situation, the Security Council has framed its resolutions not in terms of directives as to conduct but in language resembling a judicial determination of the law and of the legal consequences said to flow from the conduct of the State that is arraigned.

By way of illustration we can recall situations in which the

Security Council has responded to a situation by holding it to be unlawful, declaring it to be null and void and calling upon States not to recognize it. The principal cases in which this has happened have been the treatment of the Katanga[42] and the South West Africa[43] situations, the unilateral declaration of independence of Southern Rhodesia,[44] various facets of the Arab-Israeli conflict

---

[42] Security Council Resolution, S/5002, 24 Nov. 1961:
".....

1. *Strongly deprecates* the secessionist activities *illegally* carried out by the provincial administration of Katanga, with the aid of external resources and manned by foreign mercenaries;
.....
8. *Declares* that all secessionist activities against the Republic of the Congo *are contrary to the* Loi fondamentale and Security Council decisions and specifically *demands* that such activities which are now taking place in Katanga shall cease forthwith ...
..." (Emphasis supplied.)

[43] Security Council Resolution 276 (1970):
"...
2. *Declares* that the continued presence of the South African authorities in Namibia is *illegal* and that consequently all acts taken by the Government of South Africa on behalf of or concerning Namibia after the termination of the Mandate are *illegal and invalid*.
..." (Emphasis supplied.)

Although the *Namibia* Advisory Opinion centred upon the legal consequences for States of South Africa's continuing presence in South West Africa notwithstanding Security Council Resolution 276 (1970), the Court did not advert at all in the Opinion to the fact that the Security Council, in declaring the legal position in the paragraph of the resolution quoted above, was acting in quasi-judicial manner. Either the Court did not notice it or, if it did, appears not to have thought that that consideration affected its Opinion. In either event, the attitude of the Court does not affect the two points being made here, namely, first, that States appear to have set a very low threshhold for their consent to the exercise of Security Council jurisdiction and, second, that there is room for consideration of the desirability of providing a process of judicial review for such actions of organs of international organizations.

[44] Security Council Resolution 217 (1965), 20 Nov. 1965:
"...
3. Condemns the usurpation of power by a racist settler minority in Southern Rhodesia and *regards the declaration of independence by it as having no legal validity*" (Emphasis supplied.)

Other Security Council Resolutions contain references to "illegality". Resolution 216 (1965), 12 November 1965: "... calls upon all States not to recognize the *illegal* racist minority régime in Southern Rhodesia". See also Resolution 232 (1966), 16 Dec. 1966 and Resolution 253 (1968), 29 May 1968. Resolution 277 (1970), 18 March 1970:
"...
1. Condemns the *illegal* proclamation of republican status of the territory by the *illegal* régime in Southern Rhodesia;
2. Decides that Member States shall refrain from recognizing this *illegal* régime or from rendering any assistance to it;
..." (Emphasis supplied.)

QUASI-JUDICIAL ACTIVITY OF SECURITY COUNCIL 41

including, in particular, the status of Jerusalem[45] and the Occupied Territories, the position of the so-called independent "Homelands" in South Africa,[46] the establishment of the Turkish Republic of Northern Cyprus[47] and, most recently, the Iraqi "annexation" of Kuwait.[48]

[45] Security Council Resolution 252 (1968), 21 May 1968:
"...
2. *Considers* that all legislative and administrative measures and actions taken by Israel, including expropriation of land and properties thereon, which tend to change the legal status of Jerusalem are *invalid and cannot change that status*.
..." (Emphasis supplied.)
Security Council Resolution 298 (1971):
"...
3. *Confirms* in the clearest possible terms that all legislative and administrative actions taken by Israel to change the status of the City of Jerusalem, including expropriation of land and properties, transfer of populations and legislation aimed at the incorporation of the occupied sector, are *totally invalid and cannot change that status*.
..." (Emphasis supplied)
Security Council Resolution 478 (1980).
"...
2. *Affirms* that the enactment of the "basic law" by Israel *constitutes a violation of international law and does not affect the continued application of the Geneva Convention* relative to the Protection of Civilian Persons in Time of War ...
3. *Determines* that all legislative and administrative measures and actions taken by Israel ... which have altered or purport to alter the character and status of the Holy City of Jerusalem ... *are null and void* and must be rescinded forthwith.
..." (Emphasis supplied.)
[46] Statement by the President of the Security Council, 21 Sep. 1979, S/13549:
"The Security Council condemns the proclamation of the so-called 'independence' of Venda and *declares it totally invalid* ..." (Emphasis supplied.)
See also a similar statement made in relation to Ciskei, 15 Dec. 1981, S/14794.
[47] On 15 November 1983 the Turkish Cypriot Government in Northern Cyprus declared the establishment in that part of the island of the Turkish Republic of Northern Cyprus. Three days later, in response to a complaint by the Greek Cypriot Government, whose actual exercise of authority had for the previous nine years been limited to the southern part of the island, the Security Council adopted a resolution in which it expressed a number of views about the law. The Preamble stated *inter alia* that "this Declaration [i.e. the one by the Turkish Cypriot Government] is incompatible with the 1960 Treaty concerning the establishment of the Republic of Cyprus and the 1960 Treaty of Guarantee" and "therefore that the attempt to create a 'Turkish Republic of Northern Cyprus' is invalid". In the operative part of the Resolution the Council stated that it "considers the Declaration referred to above *as legally invalid and calls for its withdrawal*". (Emphasis supplied.) The Resolution was not, of course, limited to such expressions of legal opinion, but also contained a number of political statements and directions.
[48] Security Council Resolution 662 (1990), 9 Aug. 1990:
"...
1. Decides that the annexation of Kuwait by Iraq under any form and whatever pretext has *no legal validity*, and is considered *null and void*.
..." (Emphasis supplied.)

The question that has to be asked in the context of the administration of international justice is whether, and if so where and on what conditions, a line should be drawn between, on the one hand, pronouncements by the Security Council specifically and directly related to its task of maintaining and restoring international peace and security and, on the other, mere declarations of law. The Security Council is a political body performing political functions. It has been commonplace in describing its activities to say that it is not concerned with the law and, in calling upon parties to take measures to restore peace, is not interested in, or essentially influenced by, the degree to which any of them may have been acting unlawfully. What, then, is to be said when the Council in effect acts as a court of law – at any rate, in the sense of determining that conduct is unlawful and declaring it to be "null and void".[49]

It is evident that in reaching its conclusions about the law the Security Council has not acted in a way that would normally be recognized as judicial. Though it may have given the "defendant" party an opportunity to put its case, it certainly will not have heard evidence presented in the systematic manner associated with court proceedings; there will have been no cross-examination of witnesses; there will have been no detailed assessment of the legal background and the legal factors; and, above all, the assessment of the evidence and the determination of the law will not have been free from collateral political considerations in the same way as the process of reaching a truly judicial conclusion would or should have been. The usual procedure is that a draft resolution expressing the conclusions of the Council will have been circulated at an early stage in the debate, perhaps even before its actual commencement, and activity in the Council will have been

---

[49] There appears to have been little writing directed specifically to the conduct of the Security Council as a quasi-judicial body. But see Higgins, "The Place of International Law in the Settlement of Disputes by the Security Council", 64 *AJIL* 1 (1970) and Stephen, "Natural Justice at the United Nations: The Rhodesia Case", 67 *AJIL* 479 (1973), who draws attention to non-observance of the *audi alterem partem* rule. See also Gowlland-Debbas, *Collective Responses to Illegal Acts in International Law* (1990), esp. 265-269.

aimed at negotiating the final text of the resolution and securing political adhesion to it, rather than at reaching an impartial conclusion based upon unbiased consideration of the facts and objective examination of the law. Certainly, there will be no statement by the Council as such presenting a reasoned explanation of its conclusions of law and fact in a manner comparable to that of a judgment of a court of law.

Now, there is no doubt that in the performance of its tasks the Security Council must take certain decisions which involve determinations of law and fact. Confronted by an armed attack by one State upon another, it is bound to assess the situation and apply to it the relevant Charter provisions with all appropriate expedition. In many cases, the facts will be so clear that there can be no doubt that the situation amounts to "a threat to the peace, a breach of the peace or an act of aggression". The system cannot be criticized for authorizing the Security Council to identify such a situation. But the question should be asked: is there a line to be drawn between those determinations which it is proper for the Security Council to make as part of its activity directed to the immediate restoration of peace and those that go beyond that function by making legal determinations that are – in the vocabulary of the common lawyer – quasi-judicial?

The question is one which, though important as a matter of principle, appears to have received relatively little consideration by judges and little comment by States. It might have been expected that the ICJ would have discussed it in the course of the *Namibia* Advisory Opinion,[50] but it did not; and the Court's silence in this respect is emphasized by comparing its judgment with Judge Onyeama's Separate Opinion. In the context of a consideration of whether it was the Security Council's declaration of illegality in Resolution 276 (1970) that made the continued presence of South Africa in Namibia illegal, or whether instead the illegality flowed from South Africa's failure to comply with the General Assembly's

---

[50] *ICJ Reports 1971*, 16, 49 *ILR* 3.

resolution 2145 (XXI), Judge Onyeama said of the Security Council resolution:

> It was, in effect, a judicial determination, and it is doubtful if any power exists in the Charter for the Security Council to make such a determination except in certain well-defined cases not relevant here.[51] As paragraph 2 does not, in my view, create any binding legal obligations, it follows that paragraph 5 is similarly ineffective for founding legal obligations or creating legal consequences.[52]

Though it may not be possible to draw the line with absolute precision, one may suggest that a distinction can be drawn between prescriptions of conduct that are directly and immediately related to the termination of the impugned conduct, such as calling upon the aggressor to withdraw, authorizing collective forcible response or ordering the interruption of trade relations with him, and those findings that, though not unrelated, have a general and long-term legal impact that goes beyond the immediate needs of the situation. Into this category would fall legal findings that certain conduct is "unlawful" or is "invalid" or "null and void". Yet the strange thing is that the Members of the UN, in the 45 years of the Council's existence and activity, have only occasionally contended that the assertion by the Council of this wider power is improper or unlawful. Moreover, such dissents as have been expressed have been uttered by the States adversely affected rather than by other States attempting to take an objective view of the situation.[53]

---

[51] This reference to "certain well-defined cases" is possibly to: (i) the need for, and therefore the power of, the Security Council to make a determination of persistent violation of the Principles of the Charter prior to making a recommendation to the General Assembly for the expulsion of a Member under Art. 6 of the Charter; and (ii) the power of the Security Council under Art. 94(2) to review a judgment of the Court prior to making recommendations or deciding upon measures in respect of an unfulfilled judgment of the Court. Cf. the Separate Opinion of Judge Petrén in the same case, *ICJ Reports 1971*, 132-133, 49 *ILR* 122-123, and of Judge Sir Gerald Fitzmaurice, *ICJ Reports 1971*, 299, 49 *ILR* 289.

[52] *ICJ Reports 1971*, 147, 49 *ILR* 137.

[53] See, for example, the statement made by the representative of Iraq in the Security Council on 29 October 1990:
"... I do not mean to suggest that the Council is an international court or a judicial body ... [I]t is a political organ. Its members are not international judges ... acting and

It might perhaps be argued that, as individual States undoubtedly have the right to assert that the conduct of other States is unlawful and invalid, there is no reason why several States (i.e. the membership of the UN or of the Security Council) should not do collectively what each may do individually. The difficulty with this argument is that it pays no regard to the difference between the results intended in the two situations or perhaps to the difference between, on the one hand, collective action and, on the other, institutionalized action. When one State categorizes the behaviour of another as unlawful and invalid, or even when a number of States severally or jointly do so, that categorization binds no one except the State or States making it. It is no more than an expression of opinion. But when the Security Council expresses such a view in the context of action taken to prevent or remedy threats to the peace, breaches of the peace or acts of aggression, that view partakes of a special quality derived from the fact that it is not merely a collective act, but an institutional one under the Charter of the UN. Article 25 lays down that decisions of the Security Council are binding.[54] While of course the effect of a Security Council resolution must necessarily depend upon its operative verbs, the fact is that in many cases the determinations of law are coupled with mandatory verbs, such as "decides", "calls for" or "calls upon", requiring States to pursue or not a particular course of action. There is, therefore, a clear difference between the

---

voting without being influenced by their own national interest ... [T]he Council and its members are duty bound to observe the principles of justice and international law ... [T]he Council has ignored its obligations under the Charter to observe the principles of justice and international law in discharging its duties.
 The most elementary principle of justice demands that each party to a dispute should be given the opportunity to put forward its rights and claims as it sees them and to make clear what it deems to be the appropriate means of settling the dispute. In disregard of this principle, however, the Council preferred to adopt its resolutions without contacting or advising Iraq of its consultations. Those consultations took place in secrecy. The resolutions were adopted in a form that was akin to ultimatums calling for capitulation, rather than a form that urged peace ..." (UN doc. S/PV.2951, 29 October 1990. Reprinted in E. Lauterpacht, Greenwood, Weller and Bethlehem (eds.), *The Kuwait Crisis: Basic Documents* (1991), 139.)
 [54] For an important exposition of this provision, see paras. 113-116 of the Advisory Opinion of the ICJ in the *Namibia* case, *ICJ Reports 1971*, 52-53, 49 *ILR* 42-44.

46 CONSENT

action of States outside the institution and their same action within it.

There are at least two lines of comment that may be pursued about this confusion between the political and the judicial role of the Security Council. One relates to its relevance to the question of consent, which will be taken up immediately; the other relates to the question of review – which will be considered later.[55]

The point of present interest is quite simple: where do we find the consent of those affected by a quasi-judicial decision of the Security Council to the exercise by that organ of such a jurisdiction? Certainly there is no consent specific to the particular situation in which the power is exercised. So we either have to identify a more remote act of consent or conclude that we are in the presence of a usurped power. Either way, it will be seen, the significance of consent – in the sense in which it has been relied upon by the ICJ and other international tribunals – is much reduced.

If we are looking for the more remote consent, it is not, we may observe, to be derived directly from Article 25 of the Charter in which Members of the UN undertake to accept and carry out decisions of the Security Council – for that assumes a decision validly taken in accordance with the Charter. The consent is to be implied, rather, from Article 24, in which the Members confer on the Security Council primary responsibility for the maintenance of international peace and security and agree that in carrying out its duties the Security Council acts on their behalf. It is doubtful whether the States Members of the UN appreciated when they became Members that they were granting to the Security Council a quasi-judicial power additional to its political powers.[56] But

---

[55] See Ch. VI below.
[56] In the course of the *Namibia* advisory opinion the ICJ identified Art. 24 as the legal basis of the action by the Security Council in relation to South West Africa. The Court referred to the statement of the Secretary-General presented to the Security Council on 10 January 1947 to the following effect: "... the powers of the Council under Art. 24 are not restricted to the specific grants of authority contained in Chapters VI, VII, VIII and XII ... [T]he members of the United Nations have conferred upon the Security Council powers commensurate with its responsibility for the maintenance of international

whether appreciated or not, the fact remains that that is a direction in which the activity of the Security Council has extended. It is one that affects not merely those Members directly involved but all Members, since it has occurred with their knowledge and, in the absence of protest, evidently with their acquiescence.

One may ask whether the legal framework of the development is affected by the fact that a significant proportion of the entities affected have not been States in the strict sense but rather political entities whose claims to statehood have not been generally recognized by the international community, e.g. Katanga, Rhodesia and the Turkish Republic of Northern Cyprus. May it not be said that because at the relevant dates these entities were not accepted as members of the international community the Security Council need not feel any inhibition about the exercise of quasi-judicial powers in addition to its political powers? The answer would appear to be No. For one thing, the Charter can hardly grant the organs of the UN greater power in relation to non-Members than it does to Members. For another, in any event, on at least three occasions these quasi-judicial powers have been used in a manner adversely affecting Members: South Africa, Israel and Iraq.

No doubt the facts that the non-Members, by reason of their very non-acceptance by the international community, exercised no political power within the UN and that even the Member States were politically unpopular or "pariah" States provide an explanation in political terms of the acceptability of the Security Council action to the general body of UN Members. But it does not establish the legality of that action. Nor does the possibility (which can only be assumed) that such action will in the future only be

---

peace and security. The only limitations are the fundamental principles and purposes found in Chapter I of the Charter" (*ICJ Reports 1971*, at 52, para. 110).

Possibly, though doubtfully, the Secretary-General's statement can be read as extending to the exercise of a quasi-judicial power. The statement was made in a context that did not require such an extension to be expressed. The proposal under consideration was that the Security Council should, under the Treaty of Peace with Italy, assume certain functions in relation to the proposed Free Territory of Trieste. See *Yearbook of the United Nations 1946-47*, 382. See also Kelsen, *The Law of the United Nations* (1950), 284, n. 6.

48   CONSENT

adopted against similarly classified States or entities relieve those concerned with the functioning of the UN of their duty to reflect upon the implications of the situation discussed above. It would be a strange reversal of positions if the fundamental right to due process of law and fair trial, at long last internationally acknowledged as belonging to the individual,[57] should now come to be denied by the Security Council to States or other entities affected by its decisions!

E. NEW APPROACHES TO COMPULSORY JURISDICTION

If we accept that the particular activity of the Security Council which concerns us here is quasi-judicial and that the consent to its exercise rests either upon so remote an acceptance as the terms of Article 24 of the Charter, or else that the jurisdiction of the Security Council in this regard is usurped, what does all this signify for the concept of consent in relation to international judicial proceedings generally? It means, surely, that too much importance has been attached by States generally, as well as by the ICJ, to the need to identify in each case a specific act of consent.[58] Is it not strange that States appear willing to accept the kind of summary and relatively unregulated quasi-judicial activity of the Security Council closely touching, to use the traditional phrase, their "national honour and vital interests" while at the same time

---

[57] See, e.g., the UN International Covenant on Civil and Political Rights (1966), Art. 14: "All persons shall be equal before the courts ... everyone shall be entitled to a free and public hearing by a competent, independent and impartial tribunal established by law ..." See also European Convention on Human Rights (1950), Art. 6(1); American Convention on Human Rights (1969), Art. 8; African Charter on Human and People's Rights (1981), Art. 7(1)(d).

[58] It hardly needs saying that this is a political rather than a legal judgment. The lawyer is concerned only with the identification of what the law prescribes; an opinion as to whether the prescription is or is not good is necessarily political. In this context, however, the lawyer is certainly as well equipped as anyone else to make the latter judgment, even though ultimately, if any improvement is to be achieved, it is the politician who must recognize and implement it. And it may well be that it is even within the power of the lawyer, or at any rate of the judge, acting within the limits of permissible judicial discretion and flexibility, to move the law in the right direction by adopting in individual cases a less exigent view of the requirement of consent. But when such movement is initiated, it is important that it should be consistently pursued.

resisting the exercise by international tribunals of an orderly and reasoned jurisdiction in respect of disputes which rarely rise to the same level of political importance?

Part of the explanation may perhaps lie somewhat paradoxically in the very fact of the patently summary quality of Security Council justice compared with the procedural elaboration of traditional judicial machinery: a State may be willing to accept without specific consent a procedure that is rapid and unreasoned, but not one that is deliberate, ordered and rational. Though the proposition may seem odd, it may have a grain of truth in it. But if it has not – or only very little – then the way must surely be open to a realization by States that their collective conduct of the past 45 years in the UN and elsewhere has quite subverted the traditional political platitudes about the need for specific consent to the exercise of international jurisdiction. Unfortunately, however, the formal legal requirement of consent continues to exist because it is so extensively written into the prevailing legal texts – the Statute of the ICJ and of other institutional systems. But recent changes in political circumstances, coupled with the commencement of the UN Decade of International Law, suggest that the time may now have arrived for States to reflect afresh – and we must hope constructively – on the subject.

There is, in respect of so fundamental a concept as consent, an understandable reluctance to think afresh on the subject. "You'll never get States to change" is the common response to the suggestion that the subject is ripe for reconsideration. And certainly this is borne out by the conclusions of the latest inter-State discussion of peaceful settlement of disputes which took place in Malta in January-February 1991, within the framework of the Conference on Security and Co-operation in Europe. Here once again, notwithstanding some efforts to change the situation, there was an uncompromising restatement of the traditional position.[59]

---

[59] In the Introduction to "Principles for Dispute Settlement and Provisions for a CSCE Procedure for Peaceful Settlement of Disputes", Valletta, 8 Feb. 1991:
"Agreement, whether *ad hoc* or given in advance, between the parties to a dispute
(*Continued on p. 50*)

Nonetheless, it is incumbent upon States to reflect upon the implications of their own conduct. It is important to bear in mind that the "conduct" in question is not simply that of the State whose position is affected by the assertion of jurisdiction, the "victim" State so to speak. The significance of the development is not to be measured by the relative insignificance of some of the "victims". The true measure of the importance of any particular episode is that of the number of States that took part in it or acquiesced in its consequences. Thus, in relation to developments within the Inter-American human rights system it is the whole membership of the OAS that is legally affected by the implications of the enhancement by the IACHR of its jurisdiction. Similarly, in relation to the extension of the powers of the Security Council, it is at the least the membership of the Security Council and, more probably, the whole membership of the UN that participates in the State practice that supports the emergence of a new content to the rules of international law on the subject of consent. It is by reference to this body of practice that the debate on the subject of consent should continue, not on the basis of the persistent reiteration of dogmas that no longer sufficiently correspond with State conduct.

In pursuing the debate, it may be recalled – just by way of illustration – that in virtually every case in which a preliminary objection could be raised to the exercise by the ICJ of compulsory jurisdiction, it has been raised. Yet, in the period to the end of 1988, out of the 11 cases in which the challenge to jurisdiction failed, in all but two cases the respondent State subsequently participated in the proceedings and in all but one case complied with the judgment of the Court. What does this mean in terms of the "politics" of international litigation? It means that while States *prefer* to avoid compulsory jurisdiction if they can, they are nonetheless prepared to accept it if they must. The reason for objecting to jurisdiction in the first place – on such grounds as that

upon procedures for its settlement, appropriate for the parties concerned and the characteristics of the dispute, is essential for an effective and lasting system for the peaceful settlement of disputes."

the matter is awkward, embarrassing, time-consuming, vexatious, unfair, initiated without evident recourse to prior diplomatic negotiation or sufficient exhaustion of local remedies – does not stand as a permanent obstacle to eventual participation in the face of a legal determination that the reason is not valid. Basically, the position is that if a respondent State sees a possible escape from the jurisdiction, it will use it. But if there is no way out the State will accept the position.

States must, therefore, be asked: what exactly is the problem; why precisely can States not accept the concept of obligatory jurisdiction? The grounds for a comprehensive negative response become the weaker as one looks back upon the extensive range of jurisdiction which States have already positively accepted and, particularly, the manner in which in the context of the 1982 Law of the Sea Convention – the largest and most important international legislative text ever – States have been prepared to start from a positive notion of comprehensive compulsory jurisdiction, qualified only by certain limited exceptions principally in the sphere of economic discretion, rather than to adhere to the pre-existing system of a negative approach to judicial settlement qualified by a fragmentary adoption of limited jurisdictional obligations.

One does not have to be seen as being unduly idealistic – as being too little in touch with so-called diplomatic realities (if, in the light of what has already been identified as the remarkable State tolerance of international judicial or quasi-judicial assertions of competence, the diplomatic "realities" really are what they are assumed to be) – to propose that States should return to the consideration of the subject of compulsory jurisdiction. After all, there is nothing new about the proposal nor is it one alien to the thinking of many States. In 1920 the Advisory Committee of Jurists proposed just such a system of compulsory jurisdiction,[60] and the idea was revived at the time of the drafting of the Charter of the UN and of the Statute of the ICJ in 1945.

---

[60] See Hudson, *PCIJ*, 190 and Rosenne, *ICJ*, I, 364.

In the interval since 1945 there has been one material development that must necessarily affect thinking on the subject. In 1945 the proposed ICJ was foreseen as being almost the only significant international forum.[61] The range of special tribunals referred to earlier in this work[62] had yet to come into existence. It is evident, therefore, that looking to the future from this point, any new system of compulsory jurisdiction must now take account of the diversity of available tribunals established to meet special needs. There is no reason why these special structures should be interfered with – provided that, within the overall structure, there is always some jurisdiction before which a dispute can be brought.

What then, are the options as regards a "new system of compulsory jurisdiction"? One possibility is a complete and unconditional reversal of the present position, making all States subject to the compulsory jurisdiction of the ICJ in all classes of disputes. A second approach would be a qualified reversal of the present situation, in which States would become subject to the compulsory jurisdiction of the ICJ save in respect of disputes covered by some other obligatory and effective settlement arrangement or of disputes falling within a limited range of specified exceptions which States might be permitted to adopt.

A third option – which may be more readily attainable – would be to relate the change more clearly to the principal area of perceived erosion in the doctrine of consent, namely, the activity of the Security Council. It would be possible to build on the phrase in Article 36(1) of the Statute of the ICJ which states that the jurisdiction of the Court comprises *inter alia* "all matters specially provided for in the Charter of the United Nations", coupled with Article 33(2) of the Charter which provides that "the Security Council shall, when it deems necessary, call upon the parties to settle their disputes by such means" (i.e. means which include arbitration and judicial settlement) and Article 36(3) of the Charter which provides that "in making recommendations under

---

[61] The ILO and ICAO, however, each had limited jurisdiction over disputes falling within the range of their specialist activities.
[62] Ch. II.

this Article the Security Council should also take into consideration that legal disputes should in general be referred by the parties to the International Court of Justice in accordance with the provisions of the Statute of the Court".

There appears to be no reason why the Security Council should not adopt a resolution calling upon the parties to a dispute to submit it to the ICJ. Such a decision could be binding by virtue of Article 25 of the Charter. As the Court has pointed out in the *Namibia* Advisory Opinion, Article 25 is not confined to decisions in regard to enforcement actions but applies to "the decisions of the Security Council adopted in accordance with the Charter".[63] The Court also noted that

> the language of a resolution of the Security Council should be carefully analyzed before a conclusion can be made as to its binding effect. In view of the nature of the powers under Article 25, the question whether they have been in fact exercised is to be determined in each case, having regard to the terms of the resolution to be interpreted, the discussions leading to it, the Charter provisions invoked and, in general, all circumstances that might assist in determining the legal consequences of the resolution of the Security Council.[64]

In the light of these observations a Security Council resolution aiming at the establishment of the Court's compulsory jurisdiction is clearly not excluded, though care would have to be taken over its wording to ensure its effectiveness. For example, if the Council were only to "decide that the dispute shall be submitted to the ICJ", that would leave doubts as to the modalities of seizing the Court of the case.[65] On the other hand, the route to the Court might be effectively opened if the Security Council were to "decide that the

---

[63] *ICJ Reports 1971*, 16, 51-52, 49 *ILR* 2.
[64] *Ibid.*, 53.
[65] This formula differs from that used in the *Corfu Channel* case (*ICJ Reports 1948*) where the Security Council did no more than *recommend* that the dispute should be referred to the Court, but is still defective because it leaves open the question as to whether the matter may be submitted by one party alone or requires further agreement between the parties to achieve a joint submission.

dispute shall be referred to the ICJ for decision on the basis of an application to be submitted by the complainant State".[66]

F. EPILOGUE: CONSENT AND STATE IMMUNITY

In thinking again whether insistence on consent in international litigation is really essential, it may be helpful to consider its relationship with the doctrine of State immunity as applied in domestic tribunals. The same concept of consent, the continuing force of which on the international plane is here being questioned, is also invoked on the national plane as the foundation of the rules relating to State immunity from the jurisdiction of national courts.[67] These rules have for nearly a century been undergoing change in that the absolute immunity originally accorded to foreign States has now, almost universally, been restricted to an immunity only in respect of non-commercial acts or conduct *jure imperii*. The very fact that some immunity has disappeared within the national sphere necessarily leads one to ask whether the considerations which underlie that reduction also have some bearing on the elimination of the same concept on the international plane. The answer, it is suggested, is in the affirmative.

It is a notable feature of the otherwise laudable effort expended

---

[66] Rosenne, in his authoritative work on the ICJ, confines his discussion of the possible role of the Security Council to the effect of Article 36(3) of the Charter. However, he does not "exclude the possibility that the Security Council could use some other verb than 'recommend' and thereby reinforce the contentions that a new case of compulsory jurisdiction has been created". (See Rosenne, *ICJ*, vol. I, 343-344.)

[67] The point is felicitously put by Judge Sir Robert Jennings: "... jurisdictional immunity in the absence of waiver, and jurisdiction created by consent, are the obverse and reverse of the same coin. In either case it is State sovereignty that is the underlying *rationale* and historical cause": "The Place of the Jurisdictional Immunity of States in International and Municipal Law", in Universität des Saarlandes, *Vorträge, Reden und Berichte aus dem Europa-Institut/Nr.108* herausgegeben von Prof. Dr. Georg Ress und Prof. Dr. Michael R. Will (1987). Prof. Brownlie, in his draft resolution on the jurisdictional immunity of States, presented to the Institut de Droit International, also related the general principle of consent to the idea of the jurisdictional immunity of States in domestic courts by introducing an Art. VI, headed "The principle of consent", of which the first paragraph provided: "The above provisions are without prejudice to the operation of the principle of consent as a principle of general international law". 63 *Annuaire*, Pt. II, 87 (1990).

by States, whether individually[68] or collectively,[69] in reducing the scope of the "absolute" immunity of States so long enjoyed in so many jurisdictions, that the necessity for the retention of some degree of immunity in respect of sovereign acts has been taken for granted. Even Lauterpacht, whose contribution to the literature on this subject it is proper to single out[70] – partly because these Lectures are in his memory and partly, and more importantly, because his views have proved so influential – though identifying the reasons (but not the justification) for immunity in the doctrines of the dignity of the State and of the immunity of the sovereign from the jurisdiction of its own courts, was more concerned to identify a distinction between those parts of the doctrine that might be abandoned and those that might be retained than he was to question the underlying justification for any immunity at all. Perhaps in this respect he was doing no more than reflecting the hesitation that had up to that time marked the restrained acceptance of some measure of restriction by a limited number of States; or perhaps he was prudently exercising a caution that prescribed that such improvement as might be secured by a gradual approach would be threatened if the concept of immunity were subjected to total and comprehensive challenge.

However, since there is a degree of connection between the doctrine of State immunity in national courts and the requirement of State consent to the jurisdiction of international tribunals, it is proper that we should ask whether the retention of the immunity of States in matters *jure imperii* on the domestic plane is a justification for insistence on a comparable immunity (or requirement of consent) on the international plane and, in particular, whether the assumption that there really is a need for State immunity in the former context is valid. What would happen

---

[68] As in the United States by the Foreign Sovereign Immunities Act 1976. Text in 63 *ILR* 655.
[69] As in those European States that are parties to the European Convention on State Immunity, 1972. See, generally, Schreuer, *State Immunity: Some Recent Developments* (1988).
[70] "The Problem of Jurisdictional Immunities of Foreign States", 28 *BY* 220-72 (1951); reprinted in Lauterpacht, 3 *International Law*, 315-373.

if the immunity of foreign States in national courts were totally abolished? In theory, the way would be open to proceedings against States in respect of acts *jure imperii*. But what would this amount to in practical terms? Would it much matter if those cases that fall just on the *jure imperii* side of the dividing line were actually litigated if they otherwise lie within the jurisdiction of the Court? And would it not be true that many of the supposedly "dangerous" sources of proceedings, for example, a claim in State A against the government of State B by a person expelled from or denied entry to the latter State, would be found not to give rise to any cause of action justiciable in State A? The probability is that most actions involving acts *jure imperii* would, on the application of generally accepted rules of private international law, be dismissed either because the substantive law applicable to the matter was found to give rise to no cause of action, for example, because the *lex loci delicti* did not treat that particular kind of conduct as a wrong, or because the forum was *non conveniens*.

Indeed, it may be suggested that the widespread and remarkable acceptance by States of standards prescribed both in regional and universal conventions on human rights, coupled with the compulsory procedures for their implementation, compellingly evidences the reduction in the importance of the residue of so-called acts *jure imperii* in respect of which State immunity on the national plane exists. Given this truth, there seems to be little if any justification for any longer permitting the existence of such immunity in the domestic sphere to infect thinking about the exercise of jurisdiction over States in the international sphere.

Still more cogent in demonstrating the extent of the exercise of international jurisdiction in matters hitherto regarded as jurisdictionally sacrosanct because falling within the "reserved domain" of States is the wide range of issues over which the Court of the European Communities may exercise jurisdiction. To reply that this is the court of a regional and supra-national system where special considerations prevail is descriptive rather than argumentative; it does not answer the contention that if some States can submit to international jurisdiction in respect of such domestically sensitive matters surely they have by their conduct acknowledged the practical acceptability of a more comprehensive international jurisdiction.

If it is concern over "opening the floodgates" of litigation against States that inhibits a change in the present system, then one needs to probe more deeply the existing causes of, and restraints upon, litigation in the international sphere in those situations where jurisdiction undoubtedly exists. Despite the fact that there already exist wide ranges of international activity covered by various kinds of compulsory jurisdiction, there is no evidence that States lightly or wantonly resort to unnecessary litigation against each other – any more than individuals do within national legal systems. The constraints upon resort to unnecessary litigation – apart from those relatively few cases identified as frivolous and vexatious – are of a non-legal character: expense (especially the risk of bearing the costs of the other party if the case is lost); disinclination to take the trouble relative to the gain to be achieved even if optimum expectations are fulfilled; public exposure of the plaintiff's conduct; and the exacerbation of relations between the parties, possibly with lasting consequences. There is no reason to doubt the operation of comparable constraints – especially the last – in the international sphere. There really seems to be no functional justification for maintaining the immunity that States retain against actions instituted by other States.

CHAPTER IV

ACCESS

Our next concern is with access to international justice. Leaving aside the limitations that arise from the requirement of consent to the exercise of jurisdiction, it is necessary to consider whether there are within the international legal system any additional inhibitions upon the ability of those that require access to justice to obtain it.

Access to international tribunals poses significant issues for only two out of the three categories of entity whose procedural capacity requires consideration: (a) international organizations and (b) entities deriving their legal personality from national law (i.e. individuals and corporations). So far as the third category, States, is concerned, there is really no problem of access. As the dominant subjects of the international landscape, States have never been troubled by any problem about their entitlement to appear in international tribunals. The provision in Article 34 of the Statute of the ICJ that "Only States may be parties to disputes before the Court" manifestly affirms the capacity of States in that forum. Elsewhere, in other tribunals of a non-institutional kind created by special agreement between States, the problem of capacity obviously does not arise because the parties have by the very fact of their agreement necessarily excluded any challenge by each other to their respective procedural qualities.[1]

---

[1] Only in one situation would there appear to be some prospect of a problem – and this, it must be acknowledged, is at the very margins of the discussion. What is the procedural capacity of an unrecognized State? From one point of view, namely, that of the established State that declines to accord recognition to the unrecognized entity, there is no problem. If the entity is not recognized as a State it is not a State and, therefore, the question of its procedural capacity does not arise. On the other hand, from the point of view of the unrecognized entity claiming to be a State, the problem can be important. Art. 35(2) of the Statute of the ICJ provides that "the conditions under which the Court shall be open to other States [i.e. any non-party to the Statute] shall, subject to the special conditions contained in treaties in force, be laid down by the

(*Continued on p. 60*)

A. INTERNATIONAL ORGANIZATIONS

1. As plaintiffs

So far as international organizations are concerned, by reason of Article 34 of the Statute just quoted, they can have no standing as parties in contentious cases before the ICJ. On the other hand, they alone (i.e. to the exclusion of States), if authorized, can seek advisory opinions from the ICJ on legal questions arising within the scope of their activities. Such a request may be used as an alternative to a contentious case whether between an international organization and a State or between two organizations, or even between an organization and a member of its staff or a private party. In such cases, however, there would need to be agreement between the two sides that the procedure should be used in this

---

Security Council, but in no case shall such conditions place the parties in a position of inequality before the Court". On 15 Oct. 1946 the Security Council adopted Resolution 9 (1946) laying down the following conditions for participation by a non-member State: that it should have made a declaration (either particular or general) accepting the jurisdiction of the Court and undertaking to comply with decisions of the Court and to accept the obligations of a Member of the UN under Art. 94 of the Charter. Particular declarations have at one time or another been made by Albania and Italy, and general declarations by Cambodia, Ceylon, the FRG, Finland, Italy, Japan, Laos and the Republic of Vietnam. See *YBICJ, 1988-89*, 49. Any question as to the validity or effect of a declaration made under the terms of the resolution is to be decided by the Court.

The question, as yet never raised, is how the Court would treat any declaration that might be made by such entities as Taiwan, the South African "homelands" (Ciskei, Transkei, Bophuthatswana and Venda) or the Turkish Republic of Northern Cyprus. The question could have been raised in the past by such entities as Biafra and the Republic of the North Moluccas. In 1978 the European Commission of Human Rights held that in determining the status of the Greek Cypriot Government of Cyprus it should "follow the international practice, particularly of the Council of Europe". (See *Cyprus* v. *Turkey, Decision on Admissibility*, 10 July 1978, 62 *ILR* 5, at 72.) The Commission accorded the status of the Government of Cyprus to the Greek Cypriot regime and determined that the Turkish Federated State of Cyprus could not be recognized as an entity exercising jurisdiction within the meaning of Art. 1 of the Convention over any part of Cyprus. Since this conclusion was expressed to follow from Turkey's own submission that the Republic of Cyprus remained a single State, the case is one which was evidently decided on its own special facts and cannot be treated as a wider precedent. The correctness of judging the existence of Statehood by reference not to the facts prevailing in the area in question (namely the existence of a government in a defined territory enjoying the habitual obedience of the population) but by reference to the extent of international recognition of the entity in question is self-evidently doubtful, especially in situations where some States recognize the entity and others do not.

way. If not, there is likely to be difficulty with the doctrine established by the Court that advisory procedure cannot be used as a substitute for contentious procedures without the consent of the parties.[2] But the incapacity of international organizations as contentious litigants in the ICJ does not reflect a universal or unalterable rule of law and it is perfectly possible for an international organization to be a party to an *ad hoc* international arbitration in a dispute with a State or another international organization. For example, in 1967 an *ad hoc* arbitration was held between the Commission of the European Atomic Energy Authority and the UK Atomic Energy Authority relating to the liability to income tax of officials of the Commission seconded to work on a construction project in the UK.[3] An international organization may also be a contentious party in any other international tribunal that is not affected by a provision similar to Article 34 of the Statute of the ICJ. Thus the Law of the Sea Convention 1982 foresees the possibility of the Sea-Bed Disputes Chamber of the proposed Law of the Sea Tribunal exercising jurisdiction in disputes between a State and the Authority or between the Authority and state enterprises and natural or juridical persons.[4]

There is little evidence that the current needs of international organizations are not sufficiently met by the modes of recourse

---

[2] For the basic doctrine, see the *Eastern Carelia* case, *PCIJ, Ser. B, No. 5*, 2 *ILR* 394, and the *Interpretation of the Peace Treaties* case, *ICJ Reports 1950*, 395, 17 *ILR* 331. For an illustration of a case in which the Court identified the consent of the State party concerned, see the *Western Sahara* case, *ICJ Reports 1975*, 124, 59 *ILR* 30. See also the *Headquarters Agreement* Advisory Opinion, *ICJ Reports 1988*, 128, 82 *ILR* 225, which was in effect a decision between the UN and the United States on the applicability of the arbitration clause in the *Headquarters Agreement*.

[3] 44 *ILR* 409.
There can, of course, be private law or commercial arbitrations in which an international organization is a party. See: *Starways Limited* v. *United Nations* (1969), 44 *ILR* 433, a private law arbitration between an air charter company and the UN; *Westland Helicopters Ltd.* v. *Arab Organization for Industrialization and others*, a case before the ICC Court of Arbitration, 80 *ILR* 596.

[4] Art. 187. See also Annex VI, Statute of the International Tribunal for the Law of the Sea, Art. 20, "Access to the Tribunal": "The Tribunal shall be open to entities other than States Parties in any case expressly provided for in Part XI or in any case submitted pursuant to any other agreement conferring jurisdiction on the Tribunal which is accepted by all the parties to that case".

that are at present available to them. Despite the intensity of their activities over the past 45 years it is difficult to identify any case in which the absence of capacity to sue in the ICJ has by itself led to any injustice. The only episode that comes to mind in which – if the procedures had existed – there might have been a contentious case initiated by an international organization against a State is the one that the UN might have commenced against Israel in 1949 as a result of the assassination in Jerusalem of Count Bernadotte, the UN Mediator. But, even in that case, the possession of capacity by the UN would have been insufficient to found proceedings in the absence of consent by the prospective respondent to the exercise of jurisdiction by the Court. As it was, the principal legal problems arising out of the episode were dealt with by the Court in the Advisory Opinion on *Reparations for Injuries*.[5]

But the proposition that no harm has yet been done by the lack of procedural capacity of international organizations will not necessarily remain valid indefinitely. In one respect, at least, it is possible to foresee the desirability of the possession of capacity by an international organization to initiate proceedings. This is in the area of international environmental protection. If international measures in this field are to be effectively applied, the present responsibility of States to ensure that their territories are not used in a manner that occasions harm to other States – a responsibility which is still essentially bilateral as a matter between the State that causes or permits the injury and the State that is injured – may well have to be generalized or multilateralized, in the sense that what has hitherto been seen as a breach of a duty owed only to one State may become a breach of duty owed to all generally. It may therefore be desirable in this connection to accord to a suitable international organization the duty and the capacity to commence legal proceedings on behalf of the international community generally against the wrongdoing State.[6]

---

[5] *ICJ Reports 1949*, 174, 16 *ILR* 318.
[6] The fact that a procedural development of this kind would leave for separate resolution the question of the substantive law to be applied in such a case does not diminish the relevance or force of the identification of the need for the procedural

There would be nothing surprising in such a development. Although hitherto the ICJ has approached questions of international responsibility in terms of the identification of an interest in the plaintiff State – seeking, as it did in the *South West Africa Cases*,[7] a sufficient interest in Ethiopia and Liberia to justify proceedings against South Africa for breach of its obligations under the mandate for South West Africa or, as it did in the *Barcelona Traction*[8] case, a sufficient interest in Belgium to support proceedings against Spain in respect of the injury done to Belgian shareholders in a non-Belgian company – there has been increasing recognition that in some situations there exist duties *erga omnes*, breach of which may be pursued independently of the identification of a specific State interest. Among the examples given have been environmental and human rights questions.

As regards the environment, the international community should certainly contemplate the day when the enforcement of obligations under, say, conventions for the prevention of international aerial pollution, or the protection of the ozone layer, will take the form of proceedings initiated before the ICJ at the instance of the United Nations Environment Programme or some other agency more specifically endowed with responsibilities for securing compliance with obligations owed to the community generally. One of the merits of an internationalized, or denationalized, approach to enforcement would of course be that because no particular State would need to be plaintiff or complainant, the respondent would be unable to invoke – as the facts would so often warrant now – a *tu quoque* argument to the effect that the conduct of the plaintiff was as culpable as that of the defendant.

All this predicates, of course, an international willingness not only to extend such powers to an international organization but also to vest the use of such powers, not in a political organ of the

---

capacity of the organization. Evidently, such a development could only be brought about by treaty and any such treaty would have to complete the scheme for such litigation by establishing an appropriate cause of action.

[7] *Ethiopia and Liberia v. South Africa (Second Phase), ICJ Reports 1966*, 3, 37 *ILR* 243.
[8] *Barcelona Traction Case (Second Phase), ICJ Reports 1970*, 3, 46 *ILR* 178.

organization where the requirement of the adoption of a resolution upon the vote of States would enable collateral political considerations to exert an influence, but in an executive body of which the day to day functioning would be under the control of international officials protected from the influence of member States. For present purposes, however, the point to be noted is that such a development cannot take place unless there is a willingness on the part of States to accord a contentious capacity to an international organization before some effective international tribunal. If the unsatisfactory influence of Article 34 of the Statute of the ICJ could be eliminated, there is no reason why the ICJ should not be that tribunal.

Another sphere in which there is room for recognizing the value of according an independent litigious role to international organizations is that of the enforcement of human rights. As yet the devices for supervising the application of the various human rights covenants do not extend to according an initiative to international organizations. Perhaps such a need is the less pronounced in those situations in which there exists an invididual right of petition – especially where it is not necessary for the complainant to show a specific legal interest in the treatment of every victim.[9] But there remain important aspects of human rights protection where the initiative cannot be taken by individuals and

---

[9] The Optional Protocol to the International Covenant on Civil and Political Rights, Art. 1, limits the right of the UN Human Rights Committee to consider communications from individuals to those from persons who "claim to be victims of a violation by that State Party of any of the rights set forth in the Covenant". In practice the Committee has interpreted this as rendering admissible claims in relation to environmental matters both on behalf of the claimant herself and local residents who have specifically authorized her to do so but not on behalf of "future generations", (*E.H.P.* v. *Canada*, No. 67/1980, UN, *Selected Decisions of the Human Rights Committee under the Optional Protocol*, Vol. 2, 17th to 32nd sessions (Oct. 1982-April 1988), 20), claims by reason of close family and business connections (*Mbenge* v. *Zaire*, No. 16/1977, *ibid.*, 76) and claims on behalf of a husband (*Campora* v. *Uruguay*, No. 66/1980, *ibid.*, 90, 71 *ILR* 345). The Committee do not see this practice as amounting to an extension of the concept of "interest", but only as reflecting justification by the author of the communication of his authority to submit the communication. (*L.A.* v. *Uruguay*, No. 128/1982, *ibid.*, 40.) See also the American Convention, Art. 44: "Any person or group of persons, or any non-governmental entity legally recognized in one or more member States of the [OAS], may lodge petitions ..."

where the willingness of States to act may be inhibited by such considerations as apathy and self-interest. Many will recall with concern the inaction of the organized community of States when, during the conflict between Iraq and Iran, Iraq used poison gas, or indeed when Iraq used poison gas on its own Kurdish minorities. Arguably, the existence of an international organization with the power to commence litigious proceedings – whether criminal or otherwise – would have been unlikely to secure any change in the conduct of the wrongdoer. But the possibility that some good could come out of international judicial scrutiny and condemnation of such activity is not something which can be dismissed out of hand. Yet it is not something that can be brought about without acceptance of the capacity of international organizations to act in international tribunals. And it may be that in this particular connection the organization to which that capacity should be accorded is not even an intergovernmental organization but one which, though internationally recognized and in the Geneva Conventions made the bearer of important duties, derives its legal existence from domestic law, namely, the International Committee of the Red Cross.

There is no particular novelty in this line of ideas. The concept of an organ of an international organization that operates independently of its political organs to promote and secure specific organizational objectives is already well established within the system of the European Communities. If the Commission of the European Communities, in implementation of its duty to ensure that the provisions of the Treaty are applied, has the power in such important spheres of Community interest as transport, agriculture, fisheries and competition policy to commence proceedings in the European Court, it should hardly be regarded as juridically surprising or politically unacceptable that comparable developments should take place in the wider international community.

2. *As defendants*

The discussion has so far proceeded in terms of international organizations acting as plaintiffs. But there is need also to consider the position of organizations as potential defendants on the international plane. The range of liabilities that they may incur may not at present seem extensive. Nonetheless, in theory they can act in a manner which would give rise to responsibility either in delict or for breach of treaty. The manner in which in recent years the International Tin Council so conducted its activities that it became insolvent could have given rise not only to private law liability to its creditors for failure to meet its indebtedness but also to liability on the international plane to States, particularly non-member States, who might either directly, or through their nationals, have suffered damage.[10]

Evidently, the question of the judicial or arbitral determination of the rights and duties of international organizations cannot be resolved solely in terms of the capacity of such bodies to sue and be sued. No less pertinent are such questions as the extent of the powers given to such institutions by their constitutions, the nature of the tribunals before which proceedings can be conducted and, above all, the degree to which the parties concerned have given their consent to the exercise of any jurisdiction. Within the present context, however, it is necessary to recall that the question of capacity is a threshhold one. While it can, of course, be resolved in any particular *ad hoc* arrangement for dispute settlement involving international organizations, the considerations set out above are pertinent to the argument that Article 34 of the Statute of the ICJ should be so amended that international organizations are no longer *a priori* excluded from participation in the contentious work of that Court.

---

[10] The extended litigation in various national courts which sets out fully the nature of the activities of the Council is to be found in 80 *ILR* 24 (Malaysia), 31 (USA), 39 (UK), 49 (UK), 211 (UK) and in 81 *ILR* 670 (UK).

INDIVIDUALS AND CORPORATIONS 67

B. INDIVIDUALS AND CORPORATIONS

1. *As plaintiffs*

There has been direct access by individuals to international tribunals for at least seventy years. The various Treaties of Peace concluded at the end of the First World War established a series of Mixed Claims Commissions in which individuals and corporations had *locus standi* in respect of the classes of action (relating to contracts, debts and property affected by the war) specifically provided for in the Treaties.[11] The German-Polish Convention of 15 May 1927 relating to Upper Silesia also contained provisions enabling individuals to appear before the Upper Silesian Arbitral Tribunal.[12]

It has on occasion been suggested that individuals and corporations should have direct access to the ICJ.[13] Such suggestions were made, principally, in the period prior to the evolution of suitable procedures in the fields of human rights and investment disputes enabling many of the cases that individuals

---

[11] The Mixed Arbitral Tribunals that operated after the end of the First World War were the product not of a single instrument but of the whole range of Peace Treaties concluded at that time. Thus, the Treaty of Versailles, Art. 304, provided for a MAT to be established between each of the Allied and Associated Powers on the one hand and Germany on the other. Similar provisions appeared in the Treaty of St. Germain with Austria (Art. 256), the Treaty of Trianon with Hungary (Art. 239), the Treaty of Neuilly with Bulgaria (Art. 188) and the Treaty of Lausanne with Turkey (Art. 92). For cases, see under the heading "Mixed Arbitral Tribunals" in *ILR, Consolidated Tables of Cases Arranged by Jurisdiction, Volumes 1-80*.

[12] Over 4000 cases were brought before the Arbitral Tribunal. Kaeckenbeeck, who was for 15 years President of the Tribunal, made this significant comment in his authoritative study, *The International Experiment of Upper Silesia* (1942), 482:
"That many complaints of individuals should in the end remain unsubstantiated or prove futile cannot cause any surprise. But it would be unjust to deduce from this an argument against the right of direct appeal by individuals ... This is one of the vital lessons of the Upper Silesian experiment ... [O]ne thing remained absolutely beyond doubt: the protection of the population of territories subjected to changes of sovereignty is not and cannot be satisfactorily ensured by international organs which only the Governments themselves can set in motion."

[13] Even though individuals do not enjoy such a right, the Court frequently receives applications from private persons attempting to start cases against States. For example, between 1 April 1988 and 31 July 1989 the Court received approximately 1200 requests of this kind. See *YBICJ, 1988-89*, 166.

and corporations would otherwise have wished to bring before the ICJ to be brought before other – and for the particular purposes – probably no less satisfactory tribunals. Thus, as has already been indicated in Chapter 1, there now exist in the human rights field no less than five important international tribunals competent to review compliance with human rights standards in various parts of the world. It must, of course, be acknowledged that the total jurisdiction of these bodies does not correspond with the full range of countries bound by human rights obligations. The European organs cover only the members of the Council of Europe, but do not cover the countries of Eastern Europe comprised within the former Socialist bloc. The IACHR covers all the members of the OAS but the American Convention as such binds only the 20 States that are parties to it.[14] The right of the UN Human Rights Committee to receive petitions had by 31 December 1988 been accepted by 43 countries, of which 18 were not covered by acceptance of other jurisdictions.

While, of course, a significant number of countries are not bound by the basic human rights conventions, or if bound, have not accepted the individual right of petition, the problem in such instances is not one of any legal restriction on the procedural status of individuals but rather of lack of political will. As the number of those States that have accepted the requisite procedural obligations shows, there is no doctrinal or procedural obstacle to giving individuals a direct right of access to human rights tribunals. In this sphere, effort has to be deployed to secure wider acceptance of existing machinery rather than to establish additional remedial organs.[15]

Similarly, but perhaps not so widely, there has been a marked advance in the access that private persons, particularly corporations, may have to international tribunals concerned with

---

[14] See above, p. 30.
[15] This is not to say that there is not room for improvement in the present machinery of human rights supervision, but that is not dependent simply upon access and, therefore, falls outside the scope of consideration here.

the protection of foreign investment. The principal step was taken in 1965 with the adoption of the ICSID Convention. By the end of 1989 91 States had become parties to the Convention,[16] thus opening up the possibility that persons concluding investment agreements with those States might secure the inclusion therein of watertight arbitration clauses providing internationally protected access to arbitration. Though difficulties have developed in this connection, notably, an inclination for losing parties to seek review by *ad hoc* Committees,[17] the fact remains that private parties can now directly seek international arbitral assistance in a very important area of international economic activity. If wider use is not made of the ICSID machinery it is probably because some classes of large investors (notably, banks[18]) seem reluctant to include suitable arbitration provisions in loan agreements. Nor do the identifiable defects in the system stem from any limitation upon access to it – particularly since the adoption in 1978 of the Additional Facility Rules,[19] for these enable a large part of the ICSID system to be applied in situations where only one of the parties is a Contracting State or a national of a Contracting State.

While the ICSID system is general in its operation, in the sense that the system will operate as between any State that is party to the Convention and a national of any other Contracting State, there has also been one major example of a specialized tribunal to which individuals have been given direct access for the settlement of their claims. This is the Iran-US Claims Tribunal, established under the Claims Settlement Declaration of 1981 to which the two States subscribed.[20] The Declaration gave access to the Tribunal

---

[16] ICSID, *1989 Annual Report*, 6.
[17] See below, p. 103.
[18] Facts are difficult to come by in this connection, but such informal soundings as it has been possible to take suggest that a number of banks, believing that loan problems can really only be settled by negotiation, consider that international dispute resolution machinery does not have a helpful role to play in their operations.
[19] ICSID, Additional Facility for the Administration of Conciliation, Arbitration and Fact-Finding Procedures, Doc. ICSID/11, Rev. 1, June 1979.
[20] The texts of the relevant instruments are printed in 1 *Iran-US CTR*, 3-56.

principally to US nationals who had claims against Iran.[21] These claims were essentially of two kinds – those that involved allegations of breaches of international law by Iran or its government departments and those that were essentially contract claims involving the direct application by the Tribunal of the same law as would in theory have governed the contract if the proceedings had taken place in the courts of Iran or in a commercial arbitration. The especially pertinent element of novelty in this arrangement is that, though the Tribunal was established by intergovernmental agreement and the two States Parties each have an Agent supervising the conduct of cases before the Tribunal, the responsibility for the presentation of claims and the conduct of each case falls directly and exclusively upon the individual claimant.[22] In this respect the Tribunal marked an advance over other claims commissions.[23]

---

[21] Art. II(1) of the Claims Settlement Declaration (1 *Iran-US CTR*, 9) describes the jurisdiction of the Tribunal in terms of "deciding claims of nationals of the United States against Iran and claims of nationals of Iran against the United States". There have been a number of claims in the latter category. The Tribunal also has jurisdiction over official claims of the United States and Iran against each other arising out of contractual arrangements between them. There have been a number of such claims by Iran against the United States.

[22] The Claims Settlement Declaration, Art. VII(3), distinguished between claims of more than $250,000 and claims of less than that amount. The larger claims were to be presented to the Tribunal by the claimants themselves; the smaller claims were to be presented by the government of the claimant.

[23] Examples of Commissions in which the cases were handled by Agents:
Conciliation Commissions established pursuant to the Treaty of Peace with Italy 1947:
France-Italy, see 13 *UNRIAA*, 25 *et seq.*; Anglo-Italian, see 14 *UNRIAA*, 7 *et seq.*; United States-Italy, see 14 *UNRIAA*, 79 *et seq.*
Property Commissions established pursuant to the Treaty of Peace with Japan 1951:
United States-Japan, see 14 *UNRIAA*, 465 *et seq.*; Netherlands-Japan, see 14 *UNRIAA*, 501 *et seq.*
– Examples of Commissions in which the procedural position of the injured individual was recognized.
Italy-Peru – In 1899 Italy and Peru agreed to submit to the decision of the Spanish Ambassador in Peru a number of claims arising out of damage suffered by Italian nationals in Peru in the course of the civil war in Peru in 1894-95. Although the Agreement referred in one place to "claims prescribed ... by the Italian Legation ...", other provisions spoke of "the neutral character of the claimant" and of the possibility that "each of the claimants" might name a representative to appear before the Arbitrator. Again, although Art. 8 provided that the total amount of damages awarded

The extension of individual access to international tribunals has not, however, been limited to the fields of human rights and international investment – though the developments in these areas have clearly been important precedents for accepting such a right where the circumstances so warrant. Accordingly, it is no surprise that the Law of the Sea Convention should have given natural or juridical persons access to the Law of the Sea Tribunal in those situations where such persons might come into direct contact with the rules or organs established by the Convention. Thus, the jurisdiction of the Sea-Bed Disputes Chamber extends not only to States and the Authority or the Enterprise,[24] but also covers disputes between parties to a contract relating to the exploitation of the Area, including natural or juridical persons.[25]

However, apart from these specific advances, the general position is that the individual does not have a right of access to international tribunals. The exceptions are, of course, important, but they leave large areas – in terms both of activity and geography – uncovered. In relation to most potential internationally wrongdoing States, most individuals have no direct access to international tribunals and are still dependent upon the willingness of the States of which they are nationals to espouse their claims. Of course, individuals who are stateless are in an even worse position.

It would be easy to assert that there is little prospect of change. Yet the possibility should not be too readily or completely excluded. True, even within the framework of contemporary standards requiring consent to jurisdiction, States accord the

---

was to be made to the Italian Government, which reserved the right to give preference in the distribution to the most needy of the claimants, the Arbitrator expressed his conclusion in each case in terms of a payment to be made to the claimant. (See 15 *UNRIAA*, 393 *et seq*).

Mexico-Guatemala – In 1895 Guatemala agreed with Mexico to indemnify Mexican nationals for damage suffered by them as a result of certain acts by Guatemala in the area west of the River Lacantum. The reports of the decision of the Arbitrator suggest that the individual claimants were directly represented by their own lawyers and indicate that the damages awarded should be paid to the individual claimants. (See 15 *UNRIAA*, 3 *et seq*.)

[24] See above, p. 20.
[25] See Art. 187 (c), (d) and (e).

individual rights of access only in specific situations. But it is not possible to disregard the fact that those very situations now include the enforcement of human rights standards. As these standards expand and become more widely accepted, the prospect that the kinds of State behaviour that now most directly affect aliens – denial of justice, the maltreatment of the person and the taking of property – will fall within the scope of human rights protection. In that way, the goal of individual access to international tribunals will gradually be achieved.

2. *As defendants*

It is also necessary to give consideration to the position of individuals as possible defendants in proceedings in international tribunals. In this connection, it is necessary to draw a distinction between civil and criminal proceedings.

The only situations in which natural or juridical persons may at present be made defendants in civil proceedings have already been touched upon in relation to their positions as plaintiffs in the contexts of the European Community, ICSID and the Law of the Sea. There appear as yet to be no other areas in which proceedings on an international plane can be brought directly against individuals, though, of course, it must be borne in mind that an individual or a corporation may be made a defendant to a counterclaim in proceedings in which he or it is the plaintiff. The possibility that in due course a system may be devised involving proceedings on an international level against individuals or corporations in respect of the civil consequences of environmental pollution is not to be excluded. For the moment, however, the traditional position is reflected in such provisions as those of Article 235 of the Law of the Sea Convention which deals with the problem of individual liability (and, therefore, of proceedings against individuals) in terms of the obligation of States to ensure that recourse is available within their legal systems to secure relief in respect of damage caused by pollution of the marine environment by natural or juridical persons under their jurisdiction.

The position in respect of criminal proceedings against

INDIVIDUALS AND CORPORATIONS 73

individuals is quite different. The exposure of the individual to direct prosecution for the commission of war crimes under international law is now well established by the various trials held principally after the Second World War. The Allied tribunals fell into two categories: those established multilaterally by treaty and those established unilaterally by domestic legislation.[26] Our concern here is only with the former – and within that category there was in fact only one such tribunal, the International Military Tribunal at Nuremberg established by an agreement of 8 August 1945.[27] Once the trial of the major war criminals was concluded, the Nuremberg Tribunal ceased to exist. But the question has been raised from time to time in the ensuing years as to whether a permanent International Criminal Court should be established with jurisdiction to try not only war crimes but such other criminal acts as international law may identify.

The inclination to match on the international plane the principal component elements of the domestic legal structure and, for that reason, to see virtue in the existence of a criminal as well as a civil jurisdiction is understandable. But whether it can be achieved in the foreseeable future on anything more than an *ad hoc* basis is doubtful. For one thing, one may question whether there is or will be enough conduct of an internationally "criminal" kind to warrant a permanent or standing tribunal exclusively committed to that class of jurisdiction. While considerable effort has been devoted in the International Law Commission to the preparation of a draft Code of offences against the peace and security of mankind, it remains a fact that after nearly forty years the intermittent discussion of the subject is still far from a conclusion. Moreover, although there are certain kinds of criminal conduct which have continued unabated during the period of the

---

[26] As in Occupied Germany, under Control Council Law 10. (Law relating to the punishment of persons guilty of war crimes, etc., Berlin, 20 Dec. 1945, Allied Control Council, *Military Government Legislation*, Berlin, 1946.) See, e.g., *Re Alstötter*, 14 *ILR* 278.

[27] See *Re Goering*, 13 *ILR* 203. In contrast with the Nuremberg Tribunal, the International Military Tribunal for the Far East was set up by a Proclamation and Charter emanating from General MacArthur, the Supreme Commander for the Allied Powers in the Pacific. See *Re Hirota*, 15 *ILR* 356.

discussion, especially the initiation of aggression, there are other kinds of conduct which though originally important are now reduced or being reduced in significance, such as colonialism and apartheid.[28] However, there is no reason to assume that with the passage of time it will not be possible to secure some agreement on, if not an international criminal code as such, at least a number of specific acts that can be treated as internationally criminal.[29] But it must be recognized that the determination of whether such offences have been committed may possibly be overshadowed in some cases by political considerations. The uncertainty that will then follow is bound to make many States reluctant to participate in the system.

The difficulties will be compounded, however, when it comes to securing agreement on the type of court that is to be established – in particular on its composition and procedure, as well as on the types of punishment that it will be able to inflict in the event of conviction. There is small likelihood of international agreement to the imposition of the simplest penalty, namely, the death sentence. If the alternative is to be imprisonment, the question will be whether it will take place in an "international" prison or in a national gaol. If the former, who will manage it; if the latter, how does one secure compliance by the gaolers with their international obligations?[30]

Indeed, in casting about to find some way in which the establishment of a permanent international criminal court can be brought within the realms of reality, one is forced to ask more far-reaching questions: what will the establishment of such a

---

[28] See, generally, the review of the situation in *Report of the ILC on the work of its fortieth session*, 1988, Ch. IV, GAOR, 43rd Session, Suppl. No. 10, UN doc. A/43/10.

[29] The word "internationally" is emphasized because the pattern of condemnation of certain kinds of conduct, such as hijacking, terrorism and torture, manifests itself in an obligation on the parties to the relevant convention to seek criminal conviction within the domestic legal sphere.

[30] It will not be easy to forget the interpretation placed by France, and endorsed by an arbitral tribunal, upon its duty to prohibit two French military personnel, transferred to its custody by New Zealand after their conviction for manslaughter and criminal damage, from leaving the Pacific island of Hao for a minimum of three years. See the case of the *Rainbow Warrior* (1990), 82 *ILR* 500.

jurisdiction achieve; will it make the world a more law-abiding place; will it significantly add to the existing system of national enforcement of the criminal law? It is so difficult to give affirmative answers to these questions that further discussion of the individual as a potential defendant in criminal proceedings, on other than an *ad hoc* basis, seems to be devoid of practical value.

CHAPTER V

THE COMPOSITION OF TRIBUNALS

Of the many questions that may be considered in relation to the composition of tribunals, only two will be considered here: one is that of the use of party-nominated members; the other is the developing inclination on the part of States to use chambers of the ICJ rather than the full Court itself.[1]

A. PARTY-NOMINATED MEMBERS

It appears to be an almost invariable feature of the composition of international tribunals that they contain at least one member nominated by each party. This is true as much of *ad hoc* as it is of institutional bodies. Thus, in relation to arbitrations, the *compromis* usually provides either that each party will nominate a member or, if the members are actually nominated in the *compromis*, it will be on the basis that each party will have had the opportunity to name one.[2] In institutional tribunals, such as the PCIJ and the ICJ, judges who are nationals of the parties are not disqualified from sitting and, if either party does not have a judge of its nationality on the Court, it may nominate an *ad hoc* judge for the purposes of the case.[3] The same approach also characterizes the composition of chambers of the ICJ and of most standing conciliation

---

[1] Other interesting questions include, e.g., the adequacy and efficiency of the use of panels, as well as – in the context of appeals – the desirability or not of using appeal committees of constant, as opposed to varying, composition. In this connection one may note the developing practice within the ICSID system, of using the same persons to constitute the *ad hoc* Committee in different cases. There is also the problem of truncated arbitral tribunals which is authoritatively covered in Schwebel, *International Arbitration: Three Salient Problems* (1987), Ch. III, 144-296.

[2] As, for example, in the Arbitration Compromis in the *Taba* arbitration between Egypt and Israel. For the text of the Agreement, see 80 *ILR* 354; for the text of the Award, see 80 *ILR* 224, esp. 243, para. 9.

[3] Statute of the ICJ, Art. 31.

commissions. Only occasionally have parties to ICJ cases not nominated an *ad hoc* judge when it would have been permissible to do so. That ICSID *ad hoc* committees appointed by the Chairman of the Administrative Council do not include nominees of the Parties may be seen either as reflecting the fact that the dispute is not between two States but only between a State and a national of another State or, more likely, as a salutary indication that nomination of judges by parties is not an essential ingredient of international litigation.[4]

The advantages and disadvantages of the use of party nominees (especially in relation to *ad hoc* judges) have so often been rehearsed that it is unnecessary to recall them more than summarily. The following are amongst the points advanced in favour of the system: the belief that it engenders in States a greater confidence in the judicial or arbitral process by reassuring them that their different points of view will be adequately represented on the tribunal; the related belief in many quarters that a party-nominated member will not only support the cause of the party that nominated him but even communicate to that party information and guidance relevant to the conduct of the case; and the availability to the tribunal of knowledge of the national legal system of a party in cases where such knowledge is material (e.g. in connection with the exhaustion of local remedies).[5]

---

[4] For the use of party-nominated arbitrations in international commercial arbitration, see Craig, Park and Paulsson, *International Chamber of Commerce Arbitration* (1984), Pt. III, para. 12.04; Redfern and Hunter, *Law and Practice of International Commercial Arbitration* (1968), 171.

[5] A revelation of the degree of contact that can occur between party-nominated arbitrators and counsel for the party nominating them is provided in the extended treatment of the *Venezuela Boundary* dispute that appears in Wetter, *The International Arbitral Process*, III (1979), 3-352. Thus Sir Richard Webster, QC, leading counsel for Britain, said in a letter to Lord Salisbury on 19 July 1899: "If I have any reason to believe the tribunal is against me on this part of the case I shall endeavour to let the British Arbitrators know our view of the position". (*ibid.* 31-32). He also wrote to Mr Chamberlain on the same day: "If I find it necessary to take any independent action I shall do so privately through our own Arbitrators ..." (*id.*).

The attitude taken by the American members of the tribunal (the United States being engaged on behalf of Venezuela – see *ibid.* 3) was much the same, as is shown by a memorandum prepared by Mr Mallet-Prevost, one of the counsel for Venezuela. He recorded that during the deliberations of the Tribunal he was summoned to the hotel of

The principal disadvantage of the system lies in the dilution that it entails of the concept of judicial impartiality and integrity. If the independence of judges is assumed to be a fundamental feature of any proper judicial or arbitral system, why should it be thought necessary or proper for each party to seek representation on the tribunal? No judge should be expected to be pre-committed to the cause of the party that nominated him or to violate the arbitral or judicial oath by revealing to a party, for its assistance in presenting a case, the internal workings of the tribunal. Moreover, it is the task of counsel for the parties, rather than of the *ad hoc* judge, to argue the law and, in particular, to convey to the tribunal the content of the relevant domestic law of the parties. If the court has doubts on any matter, it can always put questions directly to the parties and that is to be preferred to the possibly haphazard technique of relying upon party-nominated judges as channels of communication.

Whatever may be the demerits of the system of party-appointed members of international tribunals, it is probable that the elements of the present system – the belief in the virtue of "having someone on the tribunal" – are so deeply engrained in State thinking that the abolition of the system is unlikely. There is, however, one feature of the system that could be altered in a manner that would both eliminate the most reprehensible features of the system and be conducive to the better performance of the functions of party-nominated members that the proponents of the system see as advantageous. That feature is the oath taken, or undertaking given, by a party-nominated member on assuming office.

At present, party-nominated members normally pledge themselves to act in the same way as do non-party-nominated or titular members of the tribunal. For example, an *ad hoc* judge of the ICJ, nominated pursuant to Article 31 of the Statute, is required to

---

the American members of the Tribunal, Chief Justice Fuller and Justice Brewer. The memorandum continues: "When I was shown into the apartment where the two American arbitrators were waiting for me Justice Brewer arose and said quite excitedly: "Mallet-Prevost, it is useless any longer to keep up this farce pretending that we are judges and that you are counsel ..." (*ibid*. 89).

make (in accordance with Article 20) the same solemn declaration as a titular judge that he will exercise his powers impartially and conscientiously.[6] The same is true, to take but one example, within the ICSID system.[7] Clearly, therefore, from the moment of taking the oath a party-nominated judge is exposed to a tension between, on the one hand, the positive requirements of impartiality and secrecy, which must exclude communication about the case with either of the parties, and, on the other, the possible, if not likely, expectation of the nominating party that the nominee will be forthcoming – albeit in a discreet manner – about pertinent aspects of the case and eventually will support the nominating party's position.

This dilemma for the nominee could be avoided if the realities[8] of the situation were recognized from the outset and the *ad hoc* judge or party-nominated member were relieved from taking the same oath as the titular or so-called "neutral" members. It can hardly be gainsaid that there must exist within the presently prevailing situation an element of hypocrisy, on the part of the titular or neutral members of the tribunal and of the party-appointed members, as well as of the parties themselves, if the party-nominated members take the same oath as the titular or neutral members. It would make more sense if the essentially representative quality of the party-nominated member were frankly acknowledged. Then the tribunal as a whole would be able to communicate directly with the parties through their nominated members in order, for example, to obtain suitable clarifications of the pleadings or of arguments developed during the oral stage of the case. The party-nominated member would not feel inhibited about giving his nominating party guidance about the conduct of

---

[6] The oath, as set out in the Rules of the ICJ, Art. 4, is as follows: "I solemnly declare that I will perform my duties and exercise my powers as judge honourably, faithfully, impartially and conscientiously". In addition, Art. 21 of the Rules requires that the deliberations of the Court shall remain secret.

[7] ICSID Arbitration Rules, Rule 6(2).

[8] For an informative discussion of the situation in the Iran-US Claims Tribunal, based in part on interviews with the judges, see Toope, *Mixed International Arbitration* (1990), 343-361.

the case or about avowedly pressing upon the tribunal arguments on behalf of his nominating party and, eventually, the party-nominated member could join in a majority award or file a dissenting opinion (as circumstances might require) that adequately reflects the contentions of his nominating party.[9] Such a member would thus become assimilated in fact and in theory to the so-called "arbitrator-advocate", also a party-nominated member of a tribunal but one whose task is quite openly to represent the interests of the nominating party.[10]

One difficulty with the suggestion lies – at any rate so far as institutional tribunals such as the ICJ are concerned – in

---

[9] There have, of course, been cases in which *ad hoc* judges or party-nominated members of tribunals have not supported the position of the parties that nominated them. When this has happened, it is not unknown for those who made the appointment to feel (or even express) disappointment. Such sentiments are quite out of place. It should come as no surprise that there are lawyers who are prepared to put their honour above the interest of the party that nominated them. But the question that must be pondered is whether it is right or even necessary that judges and arbitrators should be put in the position of having to make a difficult choice, when the conflict between the principle of impartiality and the interests of the nominating party can so easily be avoided by dropping the administration of a pledge that is functionally unnecessary and probably more honoured in the breach than in the observance.

[10] Although specific examples of this practice are hard to identify, the report of *Petroleum Development (Qatar) Ltd.* v. *The Ruler of Qatar* in 18 *ILR* 161 states in an editorial footnote that "The 'Arbitrator-Advocates' for the Ruler were Mr N.R. Fox-Andrews, K.C., and for the Company, Sir Walter Monckton, K.C.". There is, however, nothing in the arbitration clause of the concession that indicates that the party-nominated arbitrators were to act in this manner. Presumably, therefore, some further agreement, formal or informal, was made by the parties on this point. In opening the oral proceedings, the Umpire (Lord Radcliffe) addressed Sir Walter Monckton and Mr Fox-Andrews as "my colleagues in this arbitration". Sir Walter, in his opening, said: "... as you indicated this morning, my friend Mr Fox-Andrews and I are your colleagues, and although for convenience we are going to present the case of the parties by whom we were appointed, we shall, no doubt, at a later stage be fulfilling the functions which fall upon us as your colleagues and as Arbitrators in this case". At the close of the proceedings, the Umpire said: "... I do not propose to give a decision now with my colleagues, but to announce my decision in proper form ... after I have reviewed the matter ... What is the appropriate form in a case where there are two arbitrators and an Umpire ... I think we need not trouble to discuss today. We can, if necessary, have a word about the appropriate form when we are ready to make the decision public". (The above quotations are taken from the unpublished Note of Proceedings in the arbitration, 1 and 289.) The form of the Award did not, in fact, differ from that of other awards except that in referring to the arguments of the parties the Award used such expressions as "the Shaik's Arbitrator placed it on record" instead of the expression that would normally have been used, namely, "counsel for the Shaikh placed it on record". See also Wetter, *op. cit.*, 401.

82 COMPOSITION OF TRIBUNALS

reconciling the freedom thus to be accorded to party-nominated members with the position of titular (i.e. elected) judges. The latter, who will have taken the judicial oath at the time of becoming judges, are entitled to sit even in cases in which their own national States are parties. If the right of *ad hoc* judges to be partial is to be acknowledged, why should a comparable liberty not be allowed to titular judges? The answer is that it should be and that, to that end, national judges should be dispensed from their judicial oath if they sit in cases in which their national States are parties. The implications of the alternative, that judges should not sit in cases in which their national States are parties, conflicts with the basis upon which the question is being discussed here and, therefore, need not be considered further.[11]

B. CHAMBERS

One important aspect of the administration of international justice is the growing use of chambers of the ICJ. In addition to its intrinsic interest as a feature of the operation of that Court, the subject reflects two more general issues in the administration of justice: one is the ideal size of an international tribunal; the other is that of the nature of the distinction between judicial settlement and arbitration.

1. *The ideal size of international tribunals*

The question of the ideal size of international tribunals is of great practical consequence but is not one to which there is much substantive legal content. So, though it has some place in the present discussion, it will be dealt with relatively briefly.

Chambers of the ICJ represent a reduction in the judicial

---

[11] It is, of course, essential that the nominees of both parties should adopt an identical approach to their duties. One of the principal difficulties in the abortive *Buraimi Oasis* arbitration was that the British-nominated member "regarded his position as one of complete independence of the British Government" while the Saudi Arabian nominee was in fact in effective control of the conduct of the proceedings on behalf of his government. (See Wetter, *op. cit.*, 372.)

strength of that Court as applied to a particular case from a possible maximum of seventeen (on the basis that both parties appoint *ad hoc* judges additional to the fifteen titular judges of the Court) to perhaps seven, five or even three. Five (of which the party-nominated judges are two) is the most usual number. This reduction implies, to some extent, some dissatisfaction with the use of so large a tribunal as the full Court and this occasions the question of what is the optimum number of judges to sit in international proceedings.

The size of international tribunals has varied greatly in the past. Tribunals have usually been composed of an odd number of judges so as to avoid the risk of indecision amongst an even number of judges equally divided.[12] The various arbitral commissions of the nineteenth century usually consisted of three members, one appointed by each party and a third member or umpire selected by common agreement either of the parties or of the party-selected members.[13] But commissions of five members were not infrequent[14] – the best known perhaps being that in the *Alabama* arbitration.[15] Nor are tribunals consisting of a single person by any means unknown, though often that person has been a monarch.[16] The best known modern examples, though, are probably those of Judge Huber sitting as Rapporteur in the *Spanish Zone of Morocco* claims[17] and then as sole arbitrator in the *Island of*

---

[12] There have, however, been some examples of even-numbered tribunals. See, e.g., the two-member commissions established under the France-Great Britain Convention of 1815, dealing with private pecuniary claims (Stuyt, *Survey of International Arbitrations 1794-1970* (1972), No. 22) and the two-member mixed commission between Argentina and Great Britain under the Convention of 1830 (Stuyt, *op. cit.*, No. 29); likewise the commission between Great Britain and Portugal, 1840 (Stuyt, *op. cit.*, No. 35).

[13] See, e.g., the commissions under the Jay Treaty (Stuyt, *op. cit.*, Nos. 1, 2 and 3).

[14] See, e.g., France-Netherlands, 1815 (Stuyt, *op. cit.*, No. 20) Mexico-United States, 1839 (Stuyt, *op. cit.*, No. 33).

[15] (1872), Stuyt, *op. cit.*, No. 94, Moore, 1-653.

[16] The river-boundary question between the British and American dominions in North America was submitted to William I, King of the Netherlands, by the Convention of 1827 (Stuyt, *op. cit.*, No. 27); claims between Mexico and France under the Convention of 1839 were submitted to Queen Victoria even though she was then only 20 years old (Stuyt, *op. cit.*, No. 32, Moore, 5-4865); France-Great Britain (the "Portendick" claim), 1842, was submitted to Frederic-William, King of Prussia.

[17] (1923), UNRIAA, II, 627, 2 *ILR* 157.

Palmas arbitration[18] and W.H. Taft, Chief Justice of the United States, sitting in the *Tinoco* arbitration.[19] In the twentieth century the two principal international courts, the PCIJ and the ICJ, have each had 15 members. The Central American Court of Justice had five. The Iran-US Claims Tribunal has nine, but normally sits in chambers of three. The Court of the European Communities has 13 members. The European Commission of Human Rights and the European Court of Human Rights each have as many members as there are parties to the European Convention, at present 25. The UN Human Rights Committee has 15. The Administrative Tribunals of the international organizations vary: the UN has seven (but normally sits in smaller numbers); the ILO has three; and the World Bank has seven. The prospective Law of the Sea Tribunal is to have 21 members.

Amongst the factors which determine the choice of size of a tribunal, there can be little doubt that political considerations play a role. So far as pre-established courts are concerned their size is to a large extent affected by the anxiety of the membership of the international organization within the framework of which they are set up to ensure their own representation, if not permanently at any rate intermittently. The number of judges of, first, the PCIJ and, then, the ICJ was largely determined by the Root-Phillimore plan – a compromise between the dictates of representation and efficiency.[20] The size of *ad hoc* tribunals is also comparably affected by political considerations – in the sense that each party hopes for a tribunal the members of which may be supposed by reason of nationality to be sympathetic to it; and considerations of balancing one off against another may control whether the tribunal shall consist of three or five members additional to those who are nationals of the parties.

Common to all tribunals there is a functional consideration also: the smaller the tribunal the more homogeneous it is likely to be, the easier it will be to organize, the quicker it can reach its decisions

---

[18] (1928), UNRIAA, II, 829, 4 *ILR* 103.
[19] (1923), UNRIAA, I, 375, 2 *ILR* 34.
[20] See Hudson, *PCIJ*, 147-8.

and the smaller will be its cost. It is impossible to justify in functional terms the size of courts such as the ICJ, unless it be by the rather theoretical consideration that the larger the court the greater the authority that its judgments will carry. That notion, however, is fine when the Court decides by a comfortable majority, but is less persuasive when the Court divides eight to seven or nine to six.

Beyond pointing to the considerations which militate in favour of five or three-member tribunals, it is not necessary or constructive to argue in favour of a universally applicable number. But considerations of speed and efficiency, as well possibly as the negative element of excluding from the proceedings certain supposedly unsympathetic judges, helps to explain the recent recourse to chambers of the ICJ; and it is against that background that the development must in part be considered.

2. *The relevance of the distinction between arbitration and judicial settlement*

As will presently become apparent, the difference of opinion regarding the desirability or even the permissibility of the extension of the use of chambers as an expression of the preference of parties before the ICJ for a decision by a smaller tribunal over the composition of which they have exerted an influence, turns in large measure upon a lack of agreement as to the nature of the distinction between arbitration and judicial settlement.

To probe this distinction more deeply we must start from the traditional recitation of the modes of peaceful settlement. This separates, first, those methods that do not involve a determination and application of law from, second, those methods that do. One may leave aside the details of the first category (negotiation, good offices, mediation and conciliation) and pass straight to the second category. Arbitration and judicial settlement are normally placed in this class. They are customarily distinguished from each other on the basis, principally, that judicial settlement is institutionalized in the form of a pre-established court while arbitration is conducted by arbitrators specially selected for each case and thus lacks judicial continuity. But the lines have become blurred and arbitration has in a number of instances become institutionalized, as in the shape of the Permanent Court of Arbitration, of ICSID, and even of the Iran-US Claims Tribunal.[21]

There is, however, another distinction that has been drawn between arbitration and judicial settlement, to the effect that arbitration is really an extension of the diplomatic process and that, in consequence, arbitrators are freer than are judges to depart from the strict application of law.[22] Both in the PCIJ and in the ICJ there have been notable statements of this view. In the PCIJ, Judge Kellogg, in his Observations (in effect a Separate Opinion) on the Order of 6 December 1930 in the case of the *Free Zones of Upper Savoy and the District of Gex*,[23] adopted with approval the statement of instructions given by the US Secretary of State, Elihu Root, to the American delegates to The Hague Peace Conference of 1907. Those instructions said, *inter alia*:

> There can be no doubt that the principal objection to arbitration rests not upon the unwillingness of nations to submit their controversies to impartial arbitration, but upon an apprehension that the arbitration to which they submit may not be impartial; it has been a very general practice for arbitrators to act, not as judges deciding questions of fact and law upon the record before them under a sense of judicial responsibility, but as negotiators effecting settlements of the questions brought before them in accordance with the traditions and usages and subject to all the considerations and influences which affect diplomatic agents.[24]

---

[21] Though the Iran-US Claims Tribunal possesses many of the institutional qualities of a court, its awards have often been likened to arbitral awards.

[22] For a striking statement of this view, see the report in the memorandum of Mr Mallet-Prevost (referred to above, n. 5) of his conversation with Lord Russell, one of the British-appointed arbitrators in the *Venezuelan Boundary* dispute: "I sat next to Lord Russell and, in the course of our conversation, ventured to express the opinion that international arbitrations should base their decisions exclusively on legal grounds. Lord Russell immediately responded saying: 'I entirely disagree with you. I think that international arbitrations should be conducted on broader lines and that they should take into consideration questions of international policy'." (as quoted in Wetter, *op. cit.*, 88).

[23] PCIJ, Ser A. No. 24, 4, at 29 *et seq.*

[24] *Ibid.*, 36.

The same idea was echoed in the report subsequently made by the American delegation to the Secretary of State, following the 1907 Conference, when speaking of an international court of justice:

> It is obvious that such a court, acting under a sense of judicial responsibility, would decide, as a court, according to international law and equity, a question submitted to it, and that the idea of compromise hitherto so inseparable from arbitration should be a stranger to this institution.[25]

Drawing upon such statements, Judge Kellogg warned in the strongest terms against any dilution of the judicial quality of the PCIJ that might flow from its acceptance of a request from the parties in that case that the Court should formulate a special and complicated customs regime between the two States. He argued that "it is scarcely possible that it was intended that, even with the consent of the Parties, the Court should take jurisdiction of political questions, should exercise the function of drafting treaties between nations or decide questions upon grounds of political and economic expediency".[26] He perceived a critical difference between the direction given to an arbitral tribunal to decide a controversy "on the basis of respect for the law" and that given to a court to decide "by an application of principles of law". The former, as he saw it, merely started from respect for the law, but did not necessarily adhere to it, while the latter involved strict conformity with the law.

3. *The approach of the International Court of Justice in the El Salvador/ Honduras case*

The insistence upon the distinction between judicial settlement and arbitration has surfaced again in the separate opinion of Judge Shahabuddeen in the *Application for Permission by Nicaragua to Intervene in the El Salvador/Honduras Case*.[27] The issue at this stage of

---

[25] *Ibid.*, 37.
[26] *Ibid.*, 39.
[27] *ICJ Reports 1990*, 92.

the proceedings was whether the application by Nicaragua to intervene in a case, which had – at the request of the parties – been referred to a Chamber, should be heard by the full Court or by the Chamber.

In explaining the significance of the distinction, it may be helpful, first, to say something more about the Chambers system. The Statute of the ICJ contains two kinds of provisions for the use of chambers. The first relates to what are, in effect, standing chambers of the Court. Of these, there are two sub-classes. The first is the Chamber of Summary Procedure – a chamber which Article 29 of the Statute requires the Court to form. This Chamber has never been used by the present Court and only once by the PCIJ. The second sub-class consists of other standing chambers that the Court is empowered[28] (but not obliged) to establish to deal with particular categories of cases, such as labour cases or cases on transit and communications. The Court has not felt it necessary to constitute such chambers.

The second main kind of provision on Chambers authorizes the Court to form a chamber to deal with a particular case. The relevant paragraph[29] does not provide that the initiative for the establishment of such a tribunal may come only from the parties, though it does say that the number of judges to constitute such a chamber shall be determined by the Court with the approval of the parties. In fact the Court has not as yet established a chamber upon its own initiative. Instead, there have in recent years been four cases in which the parties have jointly requested the Court to make use of this power: the *Gulf of Maine* case (a maritime boundary delimitation);[30] the *Burkina Faso/Mali* land boundary case;[31] the *ELSI* case (a case about the treatment of an American-owned Italian company)[32] and the *El Salvador/Honduras* case[33] relating to the land boundary between the parties and to the status of the

---

[28] ICJ Statute, Art. 26(1).
[29] *Ibid.* Art. 26(2).
[30] Canada/US. *ICJ Reports 1984*, 246, 71 *ILR* 57.
[31] *ICJ Reports 1986*, 554, 80 *ILR* 459.
[32] Italy/US. *ICJ Reports 1989*, 15.
[33] *ICJ Reports 1990*, 3 and 92.

waters in the Gulf of Fonseca and the immediately adjacent waters in the Pacific.

In terms of the administration of international justice the developing use of Chambers is to be welcomed. Some consideration has already been given to the factors which have led States in a number of situations to prefer the use of tribunals other than the full court. Some of these factors explain why Chambers of the Court have been preferred to the full Court. Perhaps the most important is the ability that the parties are thus given to influence the choice of the judges who will sit or will not sit in the case. In this respect, it is true, the use of Chambers may be likened to arbitration rather than judicial settlement. However, it may be said in passing that there is one influential respect in which a Chamber of the ICJ can clearly be distinguished from arbitration and that is in the matter of costs. In arbitration, the parties between them have to carry the whole cost of the arbitral tribunal – both the fees of the arbitrators and the administrative expenses of the cases. In cases before the ICJ, the parties do not have to contribute directly to the salaries of the judges or the administrative cost of the Court. These expenses are carried on the regular budget of the Court which is part of the UN budget. As a result, States that want, as in arbitration, to influence the composition of the tribunal, but do not want to incur the cost of arbitration, see clear advantage in recourse to a chamber.

To return then to the application by Nicaragua to intervene in the Chamber proceedings between El Salvador and Honduras. Nicaragua argued that its application to intervene should be heard by the full Court since it was wrong that a Chamber in the formation of which Nicaragua had played no role should deal with the matter. For the Chamber to hear the application, Nicaragua argued, would run contrary to the principle of equality of States. The Court rejected this contention by 12 votes to 3, holding that the Chamber was competent to deal with incidental questions, of which an application to intervene was one. The stated precedents for this conclusion were the interlocutory decision given by the Chamber in the *Burkina Faso/Mali* case, in respect of interim measures of protection,[34] and the fact that in the *ELSI* case the Chamber had decided (albeit with the agreement of the parties) on an objection to admissibility raised by one of them.[35]

Judge Shahabuddeen dissented on a number of grounds,[36] of which the first and fundamental one was that the institution of Chambers, as regulated in the 1972 Rules of the Court, which accorded to the parties a right to be consulted about the composition of a Chamber, was really but another form of arbitration. It thus departed from the basic requirement that the ICJ act as a court. This, the Judge maintained, assimilated the Court's activity to arbitration and, since the Court was intended to be a Court and not an arbitral body, this fundamental incompatibility between the Chambers system as operated by the Court and the Court's Statute rendered the current Chambers system invalid. This position was shared, though without so great a degree of elaboration, by the Soviet judge, Judge Tarassov.[37]

By way of comment on Judge Shahabuddeen's approach, it may first be said that his objection is necessarily limited in scope. Not every case that goes to the Court is submitted to a Chamber. Of the eight cases now pending before the Court, only one is so to be decided. Nor is every Chamber open to the Judge's criticism on the ground of its composition, but only those where the parties have, by one or another means, made it clear to the Court that unless the chamber is constituted as they wish it, the case will be withdrawn from the Court and referred instead to arbitration. Prior to the *Gulf of Maine* case, for example, the US and Canada went so far as simultaneously to conclude three agreements relating to the third-party settlement of the case: in the first they agreed to refer the case to a Chamber of the Court whose members were identified in the agreement; in the second they agreed that if the Chamber was not constituted in accordance with their selection they would withdraw the case and submit it to arbitration. The third

---

[34] *ICJ Reports 1986*, 3, 80 *ILR* 450.
[35] *ICJ Reports 1989*, 42, para. 49.
[36] *ICJ Reports 1990*, 18 *et seq.*
[37] *Ibid.*, 11.

agreement contained the submission to arbitration that would operate in this contingency.[38] In no subsequent case has so open a device been used, but the fact that the 1972 Rules of the Court prescribe that the Court shall now consult the Parties as to the composition of the Chamber means that in practice the parties are consulted not only on numbers (as required by the Statute) but also on names; and their preferences appear to have been met in every case.

Now the importance of the dissenting views of Judges Tarassov and Shahabuddeen (and, to a lesser extent, of Judge Elias because his opposition to the application of the Chambers system really related to other aspects of its operation[39]) lies in the fact that the Court, being aware of the disagreement of these judges and of the grounds for it, nonetheless proceeded on the basis that the establishment of the Chamber was valid. One of the principal advantages of the expression in the Court of a dissenting opinion is that very often, and particularly when, as in this case, the reasoning of the Court is very brief, the dissenting opinion can add flesh to the Court's decision by revealing an area of discussion that evidently must have taken place during the deliberations of the Court. That the Court was able to reach its conclusion in the face of so basic an opposition as the views of Judge Shahabuddeen therefore suggests two things. The first is that the Court did not attribute the same fundamental significance as did Judge Shahabuddeen to the distinction between arbitration and judicial settlement; the other is that the Court rejected the Judge's method of reasoning.

It is convenient to comment on the second of these points first. Judge Shahabuddeen's opinion is enhanced by a wealth of learning regarding the evolution of the Chambers system and the positions expressed in the various committees, both within and

---

[38] The three agreements are all dated 29 March 1979 and are printed in the Message from the President of the United States transmitting to the Senate for its advice and consent to ratification the Treaty between the United States and Canada to submit the case to binding dispute settlement. 96th Congress, lst Session, Senate, Executive U and V, 3 May 1979.
[39] *ICJ Reports 1990*, 9.

outside the Court, that have examined the practice of the PCIJ and the ICJ over the last seventy years. His basic approach is to invoke the evidence of the intentions of the "founding fathers" – of those who initially drafted the original Statute of the PCIJ and of those who revised it in 1945. For the Judge, the issue appears to be solely, what were the words *intended* to mean? Were the parties to be allowed to control, or even influence, the composition of Chambers? The Judge's position is that language used in the drafting debates suggests that the participants did not have in mind so great a degree of involvement of the parties. Moreover, the draftsmen were still conscious of the importance of the distinction between arbitration and judicial settlement. As Judge Shahabuddeen put it:

> The question then is which shall prevail – the practical utility of a privately selected chamber claiming to be a legitimate manifestation of the Court, or the grand original design of the Court as a court of justice serving an integrated world and seen by that world to be serving it as such a court?[40]

The choice is eloquently expressed, but it will readily be appreciated that the addition to the second alternative of the words "a court of justice serving an integrated world and seen by that world to be serving it as such a court" actually adds little beyond an elegant generality to the persuasiveness of the argument. The fact is that judicial, professional and to a large extent academic opinion have ceased to be aware of, or if aware to be concerned about, the distinction made so strongly by Elihu Root in 1907 between arbitration and judicial settlement. They see little if any substantive distinction between the two techniques. To the extent that any tribunal is capable of satisfactorily applying so-called "strict" law to a case, an arbitral tribunal is expected so to do no less than a judicial body.[41] Conversely, the possibility that a Court may

---

[40] *ICJ Reports 1990*, 54.
[41] See, for example, the strictness of the approach of the tribunal in the *Beagle Channel* arbitration, 52 *ILR* 93. For the consequences of the Award, see E. Lauterpacht, "Whatever Happened to the Beagle Channel Award?" in *Le Droit International au Service de la Paix, de la Justice et du Développement: Mélanges Michel Virally* (1991), 359.

apply less than strict law to a case is now by no means excluded – as will presently be seen.

Basically Judge Shahabuddeen is pitting the strict words of the Statute against a trend, albeit insufficiently articulated, that favours settlement by any means, provided it is a settlement. Interestingly enough, he himself anticipates this criticism by quoting Lauterpacht's words in his Separate Opinion in the advisory opinion on *South West Africa – Voting Procedure*:

> A proper interpretation of a constitutional instrument must take into account not only the formal letter of the original instrument, but also its operation in actual practice and in the light of the revealed tendencies in the life of the Organization.[42]

But Judge Shahabuddeen rejected this approach by reverting to his fundamental position that an organ (the ICJ) cannot act except in accordance with its constituent instrument (the Statute). It is here, it may be suggested, that the Judge did not take sufficiently into account the fact that the Court and States have by their conduct, express and positive or implied and tacit, come to treat constitutional instruments as dynamic and evolving texts so that their strict words cease to be controlling. The majority of the Court, by not accepting the Judge's position, have impliedly reaffirmed and carried into a new field an approach which has marked the treatment of constitutional problems by this Court for the best part of half a century and which can be found even in the decisions of its predecessor.[43]

By way of example, reference may be made to one aspect of the ICJ system on which Judge Shahabuddeen would, it would seem, find himself in full agreement with the position adopted by Lauterpacht – and that is in relation to the validity of the so-called "automatic reservation".

---

[42] *ICJ Reports 1955*, 106, 22 *ILR* 651.
[43] For a survey of the cases, see E. Lauterpacht, "The Development of the Law of International Organization by the Decisions of International Tribunals", in 152 *Hague Recueil*, 381, at 414-466 (1976). See also Skubiszewski, "Implied Powers of International Organizations", in Dinstein (ed.), *International Law at a Time of Perplexity* (1989), 855.

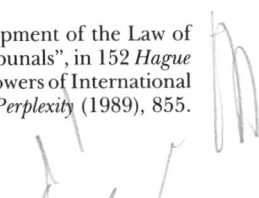

In the *Norwegian Loans* case, as already noted,[44] the difference between the majority of the Court and Lauterpacht was in the extent to which each was prepared to regard as valid the French optional clause declaration with its reservation excluding matters essentially within the national jurisdiction of France as understood by itself.[45] The Court, in deciding that it had no jurisdiction because Norway had on the basis of reciprocity used the French reservation, impliedly treated the French declaration as valid. Lauterpacht treated it as void. The division between the two sides was really one of interpretation of the Court's Statute – the Court saying in effect that almost any declaration and reservation were better than none; Lauterpacht saying that a declaration which in a given case was potentially without content was not a declaration at all. The same division reappeared in the *Interhandel* case[46] where Switzerland brought proceedings against the US alleging that the latter was unlawfully detaining Swiss property. Once more the jurisdiction of the Court was invoked on the basis of an optional clause declaration; and again one of the declarations, this time the defendant's, contained an automatic reservation. The United States did not invoke the reservation and the Court did not refer to the presence of the reservation as a ground for questioning the validity of the Declaration. Lauterpacht dissented – on the same grounds as in his *Norwegian Loans* opinion. Most recently, in the case brought by Nicaragua against the United States, neither the latter nor the Court itself showed any inclination to doubt the validity of the American declaration under the Optional Clause.[47]

We may now draw the parallel between the treatment of Lauterpacht's views on the automatic reservation and the treatment of Judge Shahabuddeen's views on the application of the Court's 1972 Rules to the composition of Chambers. Both Judges started from the view that a particular course of conduct was contrary to the letter and the spirit of the Statute. Yet

[44] *ICJ Reports 1957*, 9, 24 *ILR* 782.
[45] *ICJ Reports 1957*, 23, 24 *ILR* 784.
[46] *ICJ Reports 1959*, 6, 24 *ILR* 870.
[47] *ICJ Reports 1984*, 392, 76 *ILR* 11 and 104.

Lauterpacht's view has been disregarded by the Court on the three possible occasions on which, if valid, it should have led the Court to the contrary conclusion. Even Judge Schwebel, who before he became a judge had said in testimony to the Foreign Relations Committee of the US that he agreed with Judge Lauterpacht's position, was constrained to acknowledge in the case of *Nicaragua* v. *United States*

> that since declarations incorporating self-judging provisions apparently have been treated as valid, certainly by the declarants, for many years, the passage of time may have rendered Judge Lauterpacht's analysis less compelling today than when it was made.[48]

No State has ever raised any formal objection – by way of protest, reservation or declaration – to the validity of an automatic reservation. And though a number of States have made and withdrawn automatic reservations, a number of States still maintain them.[49]

The example given is not the only one that may be cited. Another important one is the manner in which, notwithstanding the absence of reference to reservations in Article 36 of the Statute, reservations have come to be made and accepted.

The point is of importance not only as showing that the strict wording of the Statute may not be controlling, but also – by reason of Judge Shahabuddeen's reliance upon the distinction between judicial settlement and arbitration – that this latter distinction is not one to which the Court attributes significance. The point is also of importance in relation to another aspect of the use of Chambers – and that is the question of whether they may deal with requests for Advisory Opinions. There is no provision in the Statute or the Rules of the Court expressly referring to the possibility of the use of Chambers for the rendering of Advisory Opinions and no attempt has hitherto been made to employ them in this

---

[48] *ICJ Reports 1984*, 602, 76 *ILR* 313.
[49] See Crawford, "The Legal Effect of Automatic Reservations", 50 *BYIL* 63, and Merrills, "The Optional Clause Today", *ibid.* at 114.

connection. If Chambers were to be used to give an Advisory Opinion the initiative would have to come from the Court or from the organ requesting the Opinion.

Yet it seems reasonable to suggest that Advisory Opinions – or at any rate some of them – are an area of the Court's activity very suitable for reference to a Chamber. If the ICJ is to be fully used, and retain and satisfactorily handle a case list as extensive as its present one, it does not make sense to employ the full panoply of the Court – 15 judges operating under the Court's elaborate procedures in order to reach its collegiate decision[50] – to decide, for example, whether an award of the UN Administrative Tribunal, recognizing or not the power of the Secretary-General to terminate the employment of a particular UN staff member, is correct. The case for using a Chamber to decide significant points of the constitutional law of international organizations (such as the *Reparation for Injuries* Advisory Opinion[51]) or of more general international law that arise in connection with the implementation of important political decisions (such as the *Consequences for States of the Continuing Presence of South Africa in South West Africa*[52]) may be less cogent, though not necessarily always so. In the days before UNESCO could seek advisory opinions from the ICJ on constitutional points, it referred a point of constitutional importance relating to elections to the Executive Board to a specially constituted arbitral tribunal of three international lawyers, and appears to have been content with the result.[53] But the right of the Court to use a Chamber for this purpose, appears to be in doubt.

The problem is really one of conflict between two areas of the Court's Statute. On the one hand there is a group of Articles – 25, 26 and 27 – which suggest that the Court may not sit in Chambers

---

[50] See Sir Robert Jennings, "The Collegiate Responsibility and Authority of the International Court of Justice", in Dinstein (ed.), *International Law at a Time of Perplexity* (1989), 342.
[51] *ICJ Reports 1949*, 174, 16 *ILR* 318.
[52] *ICJ Reports 1971*, 16, 49 *ILR* 2.
[53] *UNESCO (Constitution) Case*, 16 *ILR* 331. The members of the tribunal were M. H. Rolin (President) and MM. Adolfo du Costa and Lachs.

to deal with an Advisory Opinion. Thus, Article 25 stipulates that the full Court shall sit, except when it is expressly provided otherwise. Article 26, which authorizes the establishment of Chambers, speaks of their being constituted to deal with "a particular case" – the word "case" being normally associated with contentious rather than advisory proceedings. And Article 27 states that "a judgment given by any of the Chambers provided for in Articles 26 and 29 shall be considered as rendered by the Court". The use of the word "judgment" in juxtaposition to the phrase "the Chambers provided for in Articles 26 and 29" suggests that Chambers were foreseen as rendering "judgments" and, by implication, as not rendering advisory opinions. This is a formidable body of statutory provision apparently militating against the use of chambers for advisory opinions.

On the other side, there is the important language of Article 68 of the Statute:

> In the exercise of its advisory functions the Court shall further be guided by the provisions of the present Statute which apply in contentious cases to the extent to which it recognizes them to be applicable.

Can the Court not recognize as being applicable to the exercise of its advisory functions those provisions of the Statute which permit chambers to function in contentious cases? Article 68 is surely sufficiently widely formulated to be the "express" provision foreseen in Article 25(1) permitting the Court to sit otherwise than as a full Court. And the references in Articles 26 and 27 to "cases" and "judgments" are not so much a denial of the applicability of Article 68 as they are the starting point for the functioning of that article. It is an article which must necessarily assume that the provisions to be used in guiding the Court in the exercise of its advisory functions are precisely those articles which are expressed in terms of contentious cases, the ones which appear to exclude recourse to Chambers for Advisory Opinions.

The above discussion has been pursued on the basis that the question is whether the Court might *proprio motu* refer a request to a Chamber. But if the organ seeking the opinion, for example the General Assembly or the Security Council, were to add a specific request that the question be decided by a Chamber, that would tilt the scales even further in favour of the use of Chambers, since it would evidence a significant body of opinion that such a reference is possible.

CHAPTER VI

APPEALS

A domestic lawyer having considered the earlier exposition[1] of the machinery of international justice might be forgiven for thinking it strange that the international community, though apparently well-equipped with means of judicial settlement, appears to lack what seems to be a natural or inherent feature of national judicial systems, namely, a comprehensive system of appeal.

In fact, the present international structure knows of three basic kinds of recourse against a judicial or arbitral decision.[2] But before examining them it is worth recalling that there is no single concept of recourse. The idea of appeal covers a number of ways of challenging a decision: by way of a complete or of a partial rehearing; by way of reconsideration of the legal reasoning or of the facts, or of both; or by way of seeking annulment, whether total or partial, with or without a renvoi to the original tribunal, or the substitution of a new decision on the merits by the appeal tribunal.[3] The following are the types of review procedure with which the international system is at present familiar.

A. RECOURSE TO THE ORIGINAL TRIBUNAL

One kind of recourse is to return to the same tribunal to seek

---

[1] See above, Ch.1, A.
[2] An excellent brief description of appeal opportunities existing before World War II is to be found in Hudson, *PCIJ*, 430-433.
[3] See the comparative studies of various aspects of appeals by J.A. Jolowicz: "Appellate Proceedings", in *Towards a Justice with a human face: The first international Congress on the Law of civil procedure* (1977), 131-165; "Managing Overload in Appellate Courts: Western Countries", in *Justice and Efficiency, General Reports to the Eighth World Congress on Procedural Law* (August 1987), 71-94; and "Appeal, Cassation, Amparo and All that: What and Why?" in *Estudios en Homenaje al Doctor Héctor Fix-Zamudio en sus Treinta Años como Investigador de las Ciencias Jurídicas*, t.III, *Derecho Procesal* (1988), 2045-2074.

either interpretation of the decision[4] or its revision because of the discovery of some previously unknown fact of such a nature as to be a decisive factor.[5] These steps are not really "appeals" because no other tribunal is involved in the process and the original tribunal is doing no more than exercising a power inherent in its original competence – even though the power is often re-stated in the compromis. In other words, the delivery of the first award does not render the tribunal *functus officio* in respect of its original exercise of jurisdiction – or not, at any rate, until sufficient time has elapsed to make it unlikely that any such question will be raised.

B. RECOURSE TO ANOTHER TRIBUNAL

A second kind of recourse exists when there is an opportunity to challenge the decision or award before another tribunal on the ground that the award is null and void by reason of some fundamental procedural or substantive flaw. Such opportunities can arise in two ways. One is where the original agreement in submitting the matter to a court or arbitral tribunal expressly provided that recourse of this type would be possible. Such a provision, by pre-establishing the jurisdiction of the reviewing tribunal, satisfies the requirement of consent that must be met in order to establish that jurisdiction. The other is where, instead of the original agreement providing for recourse to any other tribunal, there exists a separate source for the jurisdiction of such a

---

[4] See, for example, in the judicial field, ICJ Statute, Art. 60, *Asylum Case (Request for Interpretation), ICJ Reports 1950*, 395, 17 *ILR* 339, and *Tunisia/Libya Continental Shelf Case, Application for Revision and Interpretation of the Judgment of 24 February 1982, ICJ Reports 1985*, 192, 81 *ILR* 419; and, in the arbitral field, *Anglo-French Continental Shelf Case (Interpretation)*, 54 *ILR* 139 and ICSID Convention, Art. 50. The special position of quasi-international arbitrations conducted within the procedural framework of a national legal system is illustrated by *BP Exploration Company (Libya) v. Government of the Libyan Arab Republic* (1973 and 1974), 53 *ILR* 297, in which BP considered part of the original award given by the Sole Arbitrator to be invalid and, in the absence of any provision for challenge in the arbitration clause, returned to him with a request that he reopen and continue with the arbitration. The arbitration had taken place in Denmark. The Tribunal held that the procedural law of the arbitration was Danish and that under that law the Tribunal was not competent to re-open the proceedings. BP's complaint is printed in 53 *ILR* 358. The second Award is printed *ibid.*, 375.
[5] See ICJ Statute, Art. 61.

tribunal, thus enabling an aggrieved party to make the propriety of the proceedings in the first tribunal an issue before the second one.

1. *Possibility of recourse included in the original settlement agreement*

The principal current illustration of the first kind of jurisdiction is provided by Article 52 of the World Bank Convention on the Settlement of Investment Disputes, (the ICSID Convention). The ICSID system, while not expressly providing for appeal, allows a party to request annulment of an award on the grounds that the Tribunal was not properly constituted, that it has manifestly exceeded its powers, that there was corruption on the part of a member of the Tribunal, that there has been a serious departure from a fundamental rule of procedure or that the award has failed to state the reasons on which it is based.[6] The request is dealt with by an *ad hoc* Committee of three persons selected by the Chairman of the Administrative Council from the Panel of Arbitrators.[7] Even this procedure, though a continuation of the original proceedings, is not truly an appeal because if the *ad hoc* Committee annuls the original award, in whole or in part, that is not the end of the case. The original issues may, to the extent that they are not *res judicata*, be submitted to a new arbitral tribunal.[8] The position is that, the original award having been annulled, either party is entitled to submit the original dispute to a new arbitral tribunal.[9]

There have now been two ICSID cases in which there have been annulment proceedings.

---

[6] Art. 52(1) (a)-(e).
[7] Art. 52(3).
[8] ICSID Convention, Art. 52(6). The procedure is well illustrated by the proceedings in *Amco Asia* v. *Republic of Indonesia*. An award on the merits was rendered on 20 Nov. 1984. An award by an *ad hoc* Committee on 16 May 1986 annulled the original award as a whole, though subject to certain qualifications. The case was subsequently resubmitted to a new tribunal. On 21 Dec. 1987 the new tribunal issued a Provisional Indication as to what had been annulled and what remained as *res judicata*. The matter of *res judicata* was further considered in an award of the new tribunal of 10 May 1988. (For the award of 10 May 1988, see 3 *ICSID Review* 166 (1988). For other references, see n. 13 below.)
[9] Art. 52(6).

The first is the *Klöckner* v. *Cameroons* case in which an award[10] rendered by a majority of a tribunal formerly was annulled unanimously by an *ad hoc* Committee.[11] The annulment proceedings were instituted by the unsuccessful claimant. The Committee took the view that the original tribunal had failed to apply correctly the proper law provisions in Article 42[12] of the ICSID Convention and had thus exceeded its powers. The proposition formulated by the *ad hoc* Committee was that "Excess of powers may consist of the non-application by the arbitrator of the rules contained in the arbitration agreement or in the application of other rules". It is thus evident that, at any rate on the central question of the substantive law to be applied to the case, the proceedings before the *ad hoc* Committee were effectively an appeal. They differed from an appeal only in that the Committee could not enter into the substance of certain other complaints made by the Claimant, nor – in terms of its own decision – could it decide the case on the merits. The only course open to it was to determine that the original award was null in whole or in part – and it decided in favour of total invalidity.

The second case was that of *Amco Asia* v. *Indonesia*. The original Tribunal decided unanimously in favour of the Claimant on the basis of both international and Indonesian law.[13] The *ad hoc*

---

[10] The award was rendered on 21 Oct. 1983. Extracts are printed in 10 *YBCA* 71 (1985). The Tribunal consisted of Professor Eduardo Jiménez de Aréchaga, (of Uruguay, formerly President of the ICJ), Mr William D. Rogers (of the United States), and Maître Dominique Schmidt (of France).

[11] The annulment decision was dated 3 May 1985. The full text is printed in 1 *ICSID Review* 90 (1986). The *ad hoc* Committee consisted of Professor Pierre Lalive (of Switzerland) as President, Professor I. Seidl-Hohenveldern (of Austria) and Professor A. El-Kosheri (of Egypt).

[12] Art. 42 provides as follows:

"(1) The Tribunal shall decide a dispute in accordance with such rules of law as may be agreed by the parties. In the absence of such agreement, the Tribunal shall apply the law of the Contracting State party to the dispute (including its rules on the conflict of laws) and such rules of international law as may be applicable.

(2) The Tribunal may not bring in a finding of *non liquet* on the ground of silence or obscurity of the law.

(3) The provisions of paragraphs (1) and (2) shall not prejudice the power of the Tribunal to decide a dispute *ex aequo et bono* if the parties so agree."

[13] The award was rendered on 21 Nov. 1984. The text is reproduced in 24 *ILM* 1022 (1985). The Tribunal consisted of Prof. Berthold Goldman (of France), Mr Edward W. Rubin (of Canada) and Prof. Isi Foighel (of Denmark). See also n. 8 above.

Committee reviewed the Tribunal's treatment of Indonesian law and, taking the view that the Tribunal's application of that law was wrong or incomplete, it found that the Tribunal had failed adequately to justify the amount of the damages awarded, that it had therefore failed to state reasons for the award and that in consequence the award must be nullified.[14] The case was subsequently resubmitted to a new tribunal which, in a fully and carefully reasoned decision, awarded the Claimants over $2.5 million. However, even this new award is, it is understood, now being challenged in further *ad hoc* Committee proceedings.

The conclusion to be drawn from these two cases is that a device built into the ICSID system essentially for the review of the procedural aspects of the case has become an instrument for a fresh substantive consideration of the case in the guise of examination of the award in relation to an application for annulment on certain specific and narrow grounds. As an instrument of appeal, it is clear that it is an incomplete one because the only remedy open to the Committee is to declare the original award null – a result that then enables the successful complainant (if it is the Claimant) to start the whole case afresh. The situation is, indeed, one which has occasioned a number of expressions of concern, including one by no less an authority than the Secretary-General of ICSID, Mr Ibrahim Shihata, General Counsel of the World Bank. He has observed that "if parties, dissatisfied with an award, made it a practice to seek annulment, the effectiveness of the ICSID machinery might become questionable and both investors and Contracting States might be deterred from making use of ICSID arbitration".[15]

---

[14] The *ad hoc* Committee consisted of Prof. I. Seidl-Hohenveldern (of Austria, Chairman), Mr Florentino P. Feliciano (Associate Justice of the Supreme Court of the Philippines) and Prof. Andrea Giardina (of Italy). The decision, of 16 May 1986, is reproduced in 25 *ILM* 1439 (1986).

[15] See the note by Gaillard in 25 *ILM* 1439 (1986) and the references there given to other critical studies; also Feldman, "The Annulment Proceedings and the Finality of ICSID Arbitral Awards", 2 *ICSID Review* 85 (1987).

2. Possibility of recourse arising from an extraneous instrument

The other type of recourse is where, by reason of the existence of some separate source of jurisdiction, another tribunal is able to deal with the separate cause of action arising out of the alleged misconduct of the first tribunal. Thus, provided that there exists the necessary jurisdictional link between the complainant and respondent States, the ICJ (or, indeed, any other international tribunal) could consider the validity of an arbitral award given by some other tribunal. Thus, in relation to the operation of the Mixed Arbitral Tribunals established after the First World War, Czechoslovakia, Hungary, Romania and Yugoslavia concluded a treaty in 1930 (the Paris Agreement) establishing a "right of appeal" to the PCIJ from all judgments on questions of jurisdiction or merits thereafter to be given by those Tribunals save for those enumerated in the first article of the Agreement.[16] Another example: in 1960 the ICJ examined and upheld[17] the validity of an arbitral award rendered by the King of Spain 54 years earlier in a dispute between Honduras and Nicaragua. Nicaragua denied the validity of the award on the grounds, amongst others, that the arbitrator had exceeded his jurisdiction, that the decision was insufficiently reasoned, that the award was in flagrant breach of the controlling treaty and that it was vitiated by essential error. The ICJ was able to deal with the challenge only because both parties

---

[16] Hudson, *PCIJ*, 432. Technically, the references to the PCIJ were not "appeals" in the strict sense since the proceedings in the Mixed Arbitral Tribunals were brought by individuals against State defendants whereas the proceedings in the PCIJ were brought by the national States of the individuals against the State defendants. In the *Peter Pázmány University* case, although the proceedings in the Mixed Arbitral Tribunal were brought by the University against Czechoslovakia, the "appeal" was brought by Czechoslovakia against Hungary claiming that the Tribunal had wrongly declared itself to have jurisdiction. The PCIJ said: "The fact that a judgment was given in a litigation to which one of the Parties is a private individual does not prevent this judgment from forming the subject of a dispute between two States capable of being submitted to the Court ...". (PCIJ, Ser.A/B, No. 61, 208, at 221.) See also *Appeals from Certain Judgments of the Czechoslovak-Hungarian Mixed Arbitral Tribunal*, the documents relating to which are printed in Hudson's *World Court Reports*, vol. III, 252 and the *Pajzs, Czáky and Esterházy Case*, PCIJ, Ser. A/B, No. 68, 30, 8 *ILR* 451.

[17] *Case concerning the Arbitral Award made by the King of Spain on December 23, 1906 (Honduras v. Nicaragua)*, *ICJ Reports 1960*, 192, 30 *ILR* 457.

had by special agreement accepted the compulsory jurisdiction of the Court. The review was really a new case, not a rehearing of the old one.[18]

C. INSTITUTIONAL PROVISION FOR APPEAL

The third principal means of recourse is where the institutional arrangement within which the first decision was rendered actually has built into it a provision for appeal. For example, the International Civil Aviation Convention[19] provides in Article 84 that any disputes arising out of the Convention or its Annexes shall be decided by the Council. It also provides that "any contracting State may ... appeal from the decision of the Council to an *ad hoc* arbitral tribunal agreed upon with the other parties to the dispute or to the Permanent Court of International Justice". Provision to the same effect appears in the International Air Services Transit Agreement 1944.[20] Only one case has been decided by the ICJ in which these provisions have been invoked. This was the challenge by India to a decision of the ICAO Council finding that it was competent to deal with a complaint made by Pakistan against India in the Council.[21] The Court affirmed the possession of jurisdiction by the Council. The case is of interest for two reasons. First, the Court[22] found that it had jurisdiction to decide an appeal from a

---

[18] At the present time, there is pending before the Court a case in which Guinea-Bissau is challenging an arbitral award rendered in 1989 in a case between it and Senegal relating to their common maritime boundary, essentially on the ground that the reasoning of the President of the Arbitral Tribunal (whose vote was necessary to establish a majority decision) contradicted the conclusions that he had himself reached. Here, again, the matter has only come before the ICJ because both states have accepted the compulsory jurisdiction of the ICJ, this time under the Optional Clause. Application of Guinea-Bissau filed on 23 Aug. 1989.
[19] Text in *ICJ Pleadings, Appeal Relating to the Jurisdiction of the ICAO Council (India v. Pakistan)*, 299.
[20] *Ibid.*, 327.
[21] *ICJ Reports 1972*, 46, 48 *ILR* 331. A second case is pending – an appeal in proceedings which Iran brought against the US arising out of the shooting down of an Iranian civil aircraft by a US warship in the Gulf: *Aerial Incident of 3 July 1988*, Application filed on 17 May 1989.
[22] By a majority of 14 votes to 2.

preliminary decision of the Council on the question of whether it was competent to hear the substance of the complaint (as opposed to a decision on the merits of the complaint itself). Second, although there was no discussion of what was meant by the idea of "appeal", the Court proceeded to determine *de novo* on its merits the competence of the ICAO Council, there being no suggestion that the concept of "appeal" meant anything less.

Another mode of recourse is to be found in the legal system controlling the relationship between the UN, its Specialized Agencies and their officials. Because of the immunity of these international organizations from the jurisdiction of the courts of their member States, the only way of giving staff members any form of judicial redress for complaints that they may have against the organizations arising out of their terms of employment has been by creating a special internal tribunal – the UN Administrative Tribunal.[23] Initially, there was no appeal from this tribunal, though it was always possible, if the case aroused sufficient interest, for the General Assembly of the UN (or comparable organ of the Specialized Agencies) upon their own initiative to request an advisory opinion from the ICJ as to whether a specific question of jurisdiction or even of substance had been correctly dealt with by the Tribunal. This course has never been pursued and, if it had been, it would not really have been an appeal. It could not have been initiated by either the staff member or the UN Secretariat at their sole options.[24] In 1955, however, the UN General Assembly

---

[23] The UN Administrative Tribunal serves the UN and a number of the UN Specialized Agencies. For a list, see Amerasinghe, *The Law of the International Civil Service* (1988), I, 57. The other principal administrative tribunals are the ILO Administrative Tribunal, the World Bank Administrative Tribunal and the Court of Justice of the European Communities. See generally Amerasinghe, *op. cit.*, 49-63.

[24] In 1954 the ICJ responded to a request by the UN General Assembly for an advisory opinion on the question whether the General Assembly had the right on any grounds to refuse to give effect to an award of compensation made by the UN Administrative Tribunal in favour of a staff member of the UN by holding that the General Assembly did not have such a right. (*Effects of Awards of Compensation made by the UN Administrative Tribunal, ICJ Reports 1954*, 47, 21 *ILR* 310.) This request was not intended as a challenge to any particular award and is thus not an exact illustration of the point made here.

A closer example is provided by the Advisory Opinion rendered by the ICJ on *Judgments of the Administrative Tribunal of the ILO upon Complaints made against UNESCO*,

INSTITUTIONAL PROVISION FOR APPEAL

sought to systematize the use of advisory opinions by enabling either a Member State, the Secretary-General or the staff member to request a committee of members of the UN to ask the ICJ for an advisory opinion on the matter.[25] This process is available, however, only when it is alleged that the Tribunal has exceeded its jurisdiction, has failed to exercise the jurisdiction vested in it, has erred on a question of law relating to the UN Charter or has committed a fundamental error in procedure which has occasioned a failure of justice. There have been three cases in which this procedure has been invoked but in none of them has the ICJ found the Administrative Tribunal to have been in error.[26]

Another important example of appeal, in the sense of second recourse in the same proceedings as those in which the original decision was given, is to be found in the machinery for the implementation of the European Convention on Human Rights. In this system recourse is in the first instance to the European Commission of Human Rights – by way either of complaint by a State or of petition by an individual. If the State Party concerned has also accepted the compulsory jurisdiction of the Court, then either the Commission, or the Party whose national is alleged to be a victim, or the Party which referred the case to the Commission or the Party against which the complaint has been lodged, may bring the case to the Court. This can be either by way of reference by the Commission or, in effect, by way of appeal by a State. The qualification "in effect" is added because technically many of the

---

ICJ Reports 1956, 77, 23 *ILR* 517, which, though involving recourse to the ICJ from a different administrative tribunal, was specifically related to the jurisdictional aspects of four particular cases.

[25] See Statute of the Administrative Tribunal of the UN, reprinted in Amerasinghe, *Documents on International Administrative Tribunals* (1989), 6, and Rules of Procedure of the Committee on Applications for Review of Administrative Tribunal Judgments, *ibid.*, 25.

[26] *Application for Review of Judgment No. 158 of the UN Administrative Tribunal (Fasla)*, *ICJ Reports 1973*, 166, 54 *ILR* 381; *Application for Review of Judgment No. 273 of the UN Administrative Tribunal (Mortished)*, *ICJ Reports 1982*, 325, 69 *ILR* 330; *Application for Review of Judgment No. 333 of the UN Administrative Tribunal (Yakimetz)*, *ICJ Reports 1987*, 18. The suggestion has been made that the Court has so held because it has narrowly, perhaps too narrowly, construed the grounds of appeal. See the dissenting opinions of Judges Schwebel, Jennings and Evensen in the *Yakimetz* case, *ICJ Reports 1987*, 110, 134 and 159.

conclusions of the European Commission of Human Rights which may be reconsidered by the Court are not binding.[27] So, strictly speaking, the further consideration of the matter is not an appeal. But for all practical purposes it is. The Court may rehear the case and reach a conclusion affirming, rejecting or modifying that of the Commission. There have been a significant number of cases in which the Court has differed from the Commission in its interpretation of the Convention. As a statistical example one may mention that in 1989 the Court gave 22 decisions. In six of these the Court differed from the Commission in its findings regarding the violation or not of particular articles of the Convention, a difference of conclusion which, in effect, led to a reversal of the Commission's overall findings in three of the cases.

Lastly, mention should be made of the Court of First Instance of the European Communities. The jurisdiction of this Court is limited to certain classes of disputes enumerated in the Council decision by which it was established.[28] Appeals may be brought from the Court of First Instance to the Court of Justice of the European Communities. Such appeals are limited to "points of law" which are identified as "lack of competence ... a breach of procedure ... which adversely affects the interests of the appellant as well as the interpretation of Community law by the Court of First Instance".[29] If the appeal is well founded the Court of Justice is required to quash the decision.[30]

---

[27] Not every conclusion of the Commission is a "decision". The circumstances in which the Commission "decides" matters are the following:
(i) the determination that a petition is admissible or inadmissible by reference to the conditions stated in Art. 26(2);
(ii) the rejection of a petition which is inadmissible under Art. 26(3);
(iii) the rejection under Art. 29 of a petition for non-satisfaction of the requirements of Art. 27.
Otherwise, the conclusions of the Commission take the form of a "Report" under Art. 31, which is not formally described as a "decision".
[28] This was established by a decision of the Council of Ministers of the European Communities adopted on 24 October 1988. See Court of Justice of the European Communities, *Selected Instruments relating to the Organization, Jurisdiction and Procedure of the Court* (1990 Edition), 140. The operation of the Court of First Instance is regulated by Title IV of the Statute of the Court of the European Communities, *ibid.*, 28.
[29] Article 51 of the Statute of the Court of Justice.
[30] It would seem that the whole decision must be quashed, though the Court of

D. WHETHER A SYSTEM OF APPEAL SHOULD BE DEVELOPED?

It is not necessary to consider here whether the ICSID *ad hoc* committees and the European Court of Human Rights have reached the correct conclusions in those cases where they have, in effect, reversed the forum of first instance. One must merely take note of the facts and ask this question: if, in situations where appeal is possible, there have been a significant number of reversals of the lower instance, does that suggest the existence of such a degree of international judicial or arbitral fallibility that the community should envisage permitting appeals more widely?

For some the answer will be No. They will argue that merely because the later decision rejects some or all of the earlier one is not proof that the later decision is right or the earlier decision wrong. They will say only that the second decision has by agreement been accorded a more potent effect than the first. They will point out that there is no hierarchy of tribunals in the international system and no doctrine of binding precedent which makes a decision of a higher tribunal binding upon a lower tribunal and, for that reason, more cogent. They will say too that – apart from the executive quality accorded to a particular judgment by some special institutional provision – no decision of any tribunal in the international field carries greater weight than is justified by the standing and authority of the persons who composed it or by the intrinsic quality of its reasoning. Nor will they subscribe to the view that there is an innate psychological superiority in any decision of "review" over the decision that has been reviewed. The mere fact that one person has been set in a position to pass judgment on the verdict of another does not give the second decision a greater quality than the first.

They will not deny that international tribunals are at least as capable of falling into error as domestic courts. They will acknowledge that many international decisions involve

---

Justice is empowered to give judgment in the matter, where the state of the proceedings so permits, or to refer the case back to the Court of First Instance for judgment. See Article 54 of the Statute of the Court of Justice.

questionable and appealable positions. They will note the hesitation with which States still approach judicial or arbitral settlement. Despite the history of nearly two centuries of active international arbitration, States are still not accustomed to the functioning of an international judicial system. The willingness to accept any degree of judicial settlement is, arguably, exhausted by the acceptance of a tribunal of first instance. One stage is enough. The first shall be the last and the last shall be the first. Finality is better than correctness. Ought we not to be satisfied with what we have got rather than seek further complications – especially when we already have the notion, little applied because of jurisdictional limitations, that judicial and arbitral clauses can be reviewed for procedural failure – for fraud, corruption, bias, failure to adhere to procedural rules or upon discovery of new facts unavailable at the time of the original hearing?[31]

But for others these considerations militating against appeals will not be sufficient. These others will say that every reasonable opportunity should be taken to reduce the risk of perpetuating judicial or arbitral error. A system which provides such an opportunity is to be preferred to one that does not. They will also ask a question that is difficult to answer, namely, why do we have appeals in those situations where they are available? If there cannot be appeals in all cases, why should there be appeals in any?

No satisfactory or logical answer is possible. In principle, one can say without hesitation that a system of appeal – though not necessarily a three tier one – is desirable in any system. As Warren Burger, later to become Chief Justice of the United States, said in 1968 when he was still a Judge of the Circuit Court of Appeals:

> A court which is final and unreviewable needs more careful scrutiny than any other. Unreviewable power is most likely to self-indulge itself and the least likely to engage in dispassionate self-analysis ...[32]

On the other hand, in an as yet relatively undeveloped judicial

---

[31] See, generally, Reisman, *Nullity and Revision – The Review and Enforcement of International Judgments and Awards* (1971).
[32] Quoted by Woodward and Armstrong, *The Brethren* (1979), xvii.

SHOULD A SYSTEM OF APPEAL BE DEVELOPED?

system such as that within the international community, should one not be more grateful for a willingness to accept jurisdiction at all than one is for a willingness to accept the possibility of appeals? And as to experience with appeals, of the two most active areas that we have been examining, one (ICSID) has already been criticized because the use being made of it endangers the whole arrangement of which it is a part. Of the other – the role of the European Court of Human Rights in relation to the European Commission of Human Rights – there is room for the view that the European human rights system would be better served – if only by reducing delays in disposing of complaints – by an enlargement of the primary level of compliance supervision rather than by the imposition upon a small primary level of the present system of recourse.

The choices before us are simple. One alternative is that we have no appeals at all – in the sense of review of the merits. International society appears to be ready to go one stage beyond that. Another is that we have the present unregulated and haphazard system – which is developing empirically without any real planning and may not be entirely satisfactory. The third is that we go the whole way and try to establish a proper appeals arrangement. But if we are to do that, how is it to be structured? The solution to this last question is so fraught with difficulties that we may find that, despite its idealistic appeal, it is not a practical alternative. Let us probe this a bit further.

The existence of any system of appeals, or perhaps it would be better in order to avoid any technical overtones that attach to the word "appeal" to say "recourse", reflects in large part, but not exclusively, awareness of the fallibility of judges – whether because they are careless, prejudiced, bored, ignorant or merely working under pressure. But the concept of appeal also reflects another unarticulated assumption, namely, that those to whom appeal lies are as judges in some way better than, or superior to, those whose judgment is being reviewed. If that element of superiority is lacking, appeal – except in those cases involving subsequently discovered facts, error, fraud or corruption – is merely the substitution of one person's view of the situation for that of another. How are we to choose the persons to whose views we are prepared to accord this greater degree of respect? *Quis custodet ipsos custodies?* Every aspect of an integrated international appellate system is open to sharp debate: should there be one appeal court for all international cases or should there be an extension of the present trend towards different courts for different jurisdictions; should it be a full-time or a part-time court; should appeals be by way of rehearing of the whole case, including all the evidence, or should they be limited to points of jurisdiction, of law and of fundamental procedural error; should it be a large court or a small one?

Within the scope of this work it is impossible to enter into this debate – but there is one aspect of it that deserves mention because it ties in with the consideration that we have already given to the role of chambers of the ICJ. The case for an integrated system of administering international justice is a strong one, not least in terms of the consistent development of the law. It is strongly arguable that cases are better decided by judges of experience than by arbitrators selected *ad hoc* for the purposes of a single case. Arbitration is, however, an important component of the international system and cannot be done away with. We should contemplate the possibility that its value may be enhanced if it is linked to a system of appeal. In such a system, the ICJ presents itself as the obvious principal component; and within the ICJ system, short of massive reconstruction, the device of Chambers is the one that is most likely to enable the Court to increase the dimensions of the role that it can play in the future – not least as an appellate tribunal.

E. RECOURSE AGAINST QUASI-JUDICIAL DECISIONS OF POLITICAL ORGANS OF INTERNATIONAL ORGANIZATIONS

Whatever doubts one may have about the value at this stage of international development of the already existing appeals procedures, there is one area of international activity where there is a very strong case to be made for the provision of some measure of appeal or review. This is in relation to the exercise of quasi-judicial powers by international organizations as exemplified by the activities of the Security Council which have already been referred to in Chapter III above.

Does the apparent unconcern of States with this lack of differentiation in the roles of the Security Council – that is between its role in determining the action required to restore and maintain international peace and security, on the one hand, and its role in passing legal judgment upon the conduct of one of the parties, on the other – mean that we should disregard it or accept it with complacency? No doubt it can be said that in political terms the situation seems to have been acceptable to most States. Why then seek to reform what has not been challenged? To what pressure for change would one be reacting? The answer must surely lie in a belief in legal principle and a recognition that departure from principle is capable of generating significant wrong. It is true that some of the States and entities that have been adversely affected by this approach have, in their particular political contexts, been regarded as "pariah" States. But we know enough about history to recognize that today's outcast may become tomorrow's hero. Moreover, some of the cases that have already arisen, or that may arise in the future, may well be of such a kind that a truly judicial scrutiny of the relevant facts and legal instruments would be unlikely to lead to a conclusion different from that adopted by the Security Council. Yet neither of these considerations, nor the fact that we are speaking of relatively rare episodes, diminishes the need for recognition of the problem or the desirability of the adoption of a constructive approach towards it. In the nature of things, a superficial and broad-brush approach will solve most problems. The difficult problems are the exceptional ones. They are the ones that raise significant questions of principle. And that is what we have here.

In what direction then can we move to reduce or eliminate the problem of erroneous or improper institutional quasi-judicial activity? The answer would appear to lie in the direction of judicial review; in effect, in the direction of some kind of appeal. It should be open to a State or entity prejudiced by a Security Council resolution to insist on the submission of the disputed questions of law to an international tribunal. Whether that tribunal should be the ICJ or whether, because the entity concerned may not be a State, it should be some other tribunal are matters for further detailed consideration beyond the scope of the present volume. But that States are capable of adopting collectively and within an institutional framework views that are unlawful and are, therefore, appropriate for judicial review has been shown by the episode that gave rise to the Advisory Opinion of the ICJ in the *IMCO* case.[33] Though the matter was not in itself one of prime political importance, the value of recourse to judicial review which it illustrated was immensely significant. What matters is that the ways in which one may seek a judicial verdict should not be limited to a request for an advisory opinion – a procedure that can only be put in train with the consent and cooperation of the very organ (and its members) whose conduct is being questioned. If, as indicated earlier, an international organization can assume jurisdiction over the legal issues involved in a threat to the peace, a breach of the peace or an act of aggression, so a true international tribunal should be allowed to exercise a review jurisdiction in those situations without the need for the consent of the institution concerned.

F. APPEALS AND REFERENCES FROM MUNICIPAL COURTS ON QUESTIONS OF INTERNATIONAL LAW

Before concluding this consideration of the question of appeals, there is a further aspect of the subject that warrants some attention. That is the possibility that a system of recourse to an international tribunal might be developed for cases in municipal courts involving questions of international law.[34] The idea is neither far-fetched nor ludicrous, though it is certainly easy to identify many points of difficulty in implementing it. But it is

---

[33] *ICJ Reports 1960*, 150, 30 *ILR* 426.
[34] See Schwebel, "Preliminary Rulings by the International Court of Justice at the Instance of National Courts", 28 *Virginia Journal of International Law* 495 (1988) and Rosenne in reply, 29 *ibid.* 41 (1989).

worth recalling that over eighty years ago States were prepared to accept such an idea in respect of one part of international law that at that time was actively applied in domestic tribunals – the law of prize. This, as hardly needs recalling, was the part of international law that determined the legality of seizures by a belligerent on the high seas of ships and cargo owned by enemy subjects or destined for enemy ports. Given the nature of warfare until the end of the First – indeed, even the Second – World War, prize law was a very significant part of the law of war – and it was applied wholly within the courts of the belligerents. In 1907, the Second Hague Peace Conference adopted Hague Convention No. XII relative to the creation of an international prize court to serve as a court of appeal from national prize courts. The Court, which was to consist of fifteen judges and sit in The Hague as and when summoned to deal with a case, was given jurisdiction in appeals that might be brought by neutral powers or subjects, or by enemy subjects, against judgments of belligerent courts injuriously affecting their property.

The Convention was remarkably progressive for its time – in particular in according to individuals a direct right of access to the Court. Unfortunately the Convention never secured any ratifications and did not enter into force, not so much because of its novel features but because agreement could not be reached at the London Naval Conference that soon followed it on the content of certain central rules relating to the law of prize.

The fact that this precedent for the use of an international court as a means of recourse from decisions of domestic courts on points of international law did not become operative does not mean that the idea is unsound or lacking in contemporary relevance. There are many aspects of international law on which domestic courts may be called upon to decide: the legal position of entities and authorities claiming to be foreign States or Governments, the entitlement of successor authorities to property of foreign States and Governments, the proper limits of the exercise of jurisdiction by foreign States, the immunities of foreign States and their Governments and representatives, and the interpretation of treaties, to mention but a few. And this recital does not include those issues that most often give rise to the operation of the pernicious doctrines of "Act of State" and so-called "judicial restraint", when municipal courts decline to decide controlling issues of international law that properly arise before them because they affect foreign States and are not limited solely to matters of domestic law. Principal among these are the validity of foreign nationalization decrees and questions relating to title to areas of foreign territory or continental shelf. In these cases where domestic courts are prepared to apply international law, they sometimes apply a rather "nationalist" interpretation of the law or, perhaps because of unfamiliarity with the subject, simply get it wrong. And where they decline to decide the case on the ground of Act of State or something similar, it is because they are hesitant to assume what amounts to a *de facto* jurisdiction over the conduct of foreign States. It is clearly a matter for consideration, whether it would be helpful if, in either or both of these categories of cases, a procedure were to exist under which either an appeal would lie, or a reference comparable to one under Article 177 of the European Community Treaty could be made, to an international tribunal vested with appropriate jurisdiction. The arguments in favour go principally to the substance of the matter – in particular that it would do away with the present gap in the efficacy of domestic tribunals in Act of State situations. The arguments against tend to be mainly of a procedural kind, such as additional delay in the proceedings. On the whole, once the shock of the concept has worn off, the substantive advantages should be seen to prevail over the procedural difficulties – ones which are no greater than those that arise in connection with Article 177 references within the context of the European Communities system.

CHAPTER VII

EQUITY

We come now to the application of equity and equitable principles by international tribunals, a subject which touches the administration of international justice in a number of important ways – some beneficial, others less so.[1] On the one hand, it introduces into the system a degree of flexibility. It enables the judge or arbitrator more easily to perform a constructive role in the application of the law. On the other hand, it carries with it a large element of subjectivity, unpredictability and even arbitrariness – all of which are clearly unsatisfactory.

Our task is to specify more clearly the nature of this phenomenon, to identify the role that it has come to play in the work of tribunals and to assess whether current procedures are adequate to meet the requirements for its proper application.

A. SOME CLARIFICATIONS

1. *The meaning of "equity" and "equitable principles"*

First, a word of clarification is required regarding the sense in which the terms "equity" and "equitable principles" are used here.

---

[1] There is a vast literature on the subject of equity in international law and no useful purpose would be served by attempting to provide even a selective list here. Special mention should, nonetheless, be made of the chapter on " 'Equity' in International Adjudication" in Jenks, *The Prospects of International Adjudication* (1964), 316-427, which, though written before the developments which are the principal subject of comment in this chapter, presents in detail the range of "traditional" reflections of equity in international law. See also Munkman, "Adjudication and Adjustment – International Judicial Decision and the Settlement of Territorial and Boundary Disputes", 46 *BYIL* 88 (1972-3) for a most important demonstration of the place of equity in litigation relating to territory and boundaries; and the section on "The Role of Equity in International Law", in Thirlway, "The Law and Procedure of the International Court of Justice 1960-1989", 60 *BYIL* 1, 49 (1989).

They are intended to refer to elements in legal decision which have no objectively identifiable normative content. They are, in the present context, virtually synonymous with "fair" or "reasonable". The concepts have no meaning in isolation from the details of the particular factual situation in which they fall to be applied.

In this sense, therefore, equity and equitable principles are clearly to be distinguished from the same words when used to describe certain rules of existing law. When, for example, Judge Hudson said in his separate opinion in the case of the *Diversion of Water from the River Meuse* that "what are widely known as principles of equity have long been considered to constitute a part of international law",[2] he evidently had in mind the category of specific rules of national law which pass under the heading "principles of equity". Thus the one which he particularly invoked was "that where two parties have assumed an identical or a reciprocal obligation, one party which is engaged in a continuing non-performance of that obligation should not be permitted to take advantage of a similar non-performance of that obligation by the other party".[3] The principle thus stated is no doubt fair and reasonable; but it also has a specific content which does not vary according to the factual context in which it falls to be applied. With this kind of "principle of equity" or "equity" we are not here concerned. Our interest lies, instead, in something vaguer and more relative, more closely comparable with the concept of *ex aequo et bono* as it appears in Article 38(2) of the Statute of the ICJ. Viewed thus, there is no need here to draw a distinction between equity and equitable principles. The elasticity of the concepts is such that for practical purposes the problem of applying one is much the same as the problem of applying the other.

2. *The nature of the bodies applying equity*

It will be observed in several of the examples considered in this

---

[2] (1937), PCIJ, Ser. A/B, No. 70, 4, 76, 8 *ILR* 444.
[3] *Ibid.*, 77. This is what some authors call "equity *secundum legem*". See Thirlway, *International Customary Law and Codification*, 95.

chapter that the third party upon whom falls the task of applying equity or equitable principles, though usually properly described as a judge or arbitrator, on occasion might more correctly be described as a mediator or conciliator. Also the form in which the equitable conclusion is expressed is not always that of a judgment binding in law but sometimes assumes the character of recommendations or proposals. Some may see in this manner of presentation an appearance of confusion, in that judges should be clearly distinguished from mediators and binding decisions from mere suggestions. To some extent such observations may be well founded. But though not disregarding the virtues of precise analysis, we are bound to note that in this chapter we are concerned with a feature that affects all techniques of third party settlement (whether called arbitration, judicial settlement, conciliation or mediation), namely, the adjustment of strictly legal criteria of determination to meet non-legal considerations affecting the resolution of the dispute. Provided, therefore, that we appreciate that we may not always be associating or comparing like with like, there is value in bringing together in this way some elements in the range of situations in which non-legal or equitable considerations play a role.

B. MODES OF INTRODUCING EQUITY INTO INTERNATIONAL ADJUDICATION

There are basically two ways in which equity in this broad and elastic sense can find its way into the international legal system.

The first possibility is that a treaty or a rule of customary international law may prescribe the application of a rule which is itself expressed in terms of "equity" or "equitable principles" or even of fair or just or reasonable treatment. All these formulae are inherently identical in that the result that they prescribe is not specifically elaborated. Instead the judge is called upon to construct a solution out of whole cloth according to the needs of the case. True, there may be precedents bearing on the situation, but they do not control the outcome. The judge is effectively given the task of the lawmaker – at any rate as between the parties. This is "equity prescribed by law".[4] It hardly needs emphasizing that if a tribunal purports to apply equity within, or prescribed by, the law, there must indeed be a clear basis in the law for such an application. As we shall presently see, the justification in *law* for the invocation of equity in a number of important recent cases is far from clear.

The second way in which "equity" can find its way into the international legal system is when the tribunal is specifically requested to apply equity or equitable principles *outside* the existing law and in this way to create new law for the parties.[5] The most familiar, but curiously the least used, way in which this can be done is by requiring the tribunal to decide a case *ex aequo et bono*, as provided in Article 38(2) of the Statute of the ICJ.

1. *By operation of law*

   a. *Treaty*

We may start, then, with some reference to treaties which use the standards of "equity" or "equitable principles" as a substitute for specific legal requirements.

Perhaps the most prominent text of this kind is the 1982 Convention on the Law of the Sea. Here use is made of "equity" in at least six different places.

It appears, firstly, in those provisions dealing with the delimitation of the economic zone[6] and the continental shelf.[7] In both places the rule is expressed thus: "The delimitation ... shall be effected by agreement on the basis of international law ... in order to achieve an equitable solution."

We also find references to equity in the provisions which deal with the sharing of revenues derived from areas more than 200 miles distant from the coast. The Convention contains two important novel features. Firstly, there is the requirement that

---

[4] This is sometimes called "equity *praeter legem*".
[5] This is sometimes called "equity *contra legem*".
[6] Art. 74(1).
[7] Art. 83(1).

coastal States should share with the International Authority the revenues that are to be derived from the continental shelf lying beyond 200 miles from the coast. These are then to be distributed by the Authority amongst the Parties to the Convention "on the basis of equitable sharing criteria, taking into account the interests and needs of developing States, particularly the least developed and the land-locked among them".[8] Secondly, there is the requirement that the International Seabed Authority should distribute on the basis of equitable sharing criteria the profits that are to be derived from activities in the deep seabed lying beyond areas of national jurisdiction.[9]

A third reference to equity is to be found in the provisions on the composition of the organs of the International Seabed Authority which invoke the concept of an equitable geographical distribution.[10] Fourthly, there is a provision in which rights are given to landlocked States and to developing countries which do not have an economic zone but are in the same region as other countries that do have an economic zone. Both those categories of States are to have the right to participate on an equitable basis in the use of adjacent economic zones.[11]

Fifthly, there is in Article 59 a remarkable provision entitled "Basis for the resolution of conflicts regarding the attribution of rights and jurisdiction in the exclusive economic zone". This provides:

> In cases when the Convention does not attribute rights or jurisdiction to the coastal State or to other States within the exclusive economic zone, and a conflict arises between the interests[12] of the coastal State and any other State or States, the conflict should[13] be resolved on the basis of equity and in the light of all the relevant circumstances, taking into account the respective importance of the interests involved to the parties as well as to the international community as a whole.

---

[8] Art. 82(4).
[9] Art. 160(2)(g).
[10] Art. 161(1)(e).
[11] Arts. 69(1) and 70(1).
[12] Note, not the "rights".
[13] Note, "should", not "shall".

Lastly, one may mention the provisions on transfer of technology. States are required to endeavour to foster favourable economic and legal conditions for the transfer of marine technology for the benefit of all parties concerned on an equitable basis.[14]

Nor is reference to equity limited to multilateral treaties. We find, for example, that in many bilateral treaties the standard of treatment which is to be accorded by each of the parties to the nationals of the others is that of "fair and equitable" treatment.[15] Everybody appreciates that there is no intrinsic or objective concept of equity applicable in those circumstances, but that we are there dealing with a concept the content of which is closely related to the specific facts of any given case.

We may properly ask ourselves why States deliberately resort in treaties to standards of such imprecise and unpredictable content as "equity" and "equitable principles".

Although recourse to an undefined equity may be the subject of criticism, the use of this mechanism is not necessarily a bad thing. It is all too easy, when separated from the realities of international negotiation, to point to the defects and limitations of the introduction of a reference to equity and to assert that it does not serve the cause of predictability in the law. But that kind of approach must be tempered by the appreciation that the very fact that States are prepared to have recourse to equity in a particular situation cannot be treated as a mere nothing or as an idle substitute for the vigorous tackling of a problem. It must be taken to signify something. In truth, it represents a deliberate attempt to solve a problem by blunting the sharp edges of controversy, albeit in what the outside observer may identify as an inadequate manner. But we must not be so idealistic as to deny that even a poor result in negotiation is better than none at all. And that is true

---

[14] Art. 266(3). Other earlier examples include the OECD Code of Liberalization which provides in Art. 5 that "if sufficient reasons of national importance or equity justify such a course...[a member need not take liberalization measures]."

[15] For examples see Wilson, *United States Commercial Treaties and International Law* (1960), 9, 118, 120, 123 and 154.

especially if that specific result is itself an element in helping to resolve other related and perhaps more difficult problems in the negotiation.

Nowhere is this more true than in the case of Article 59 of the 1982 Law of the Sea Convention – the provision which refers to the resolution of conflicts of interest when there is a problem of attribution of rights in the economic zone. At the stage of the Law of the Sea Conference at which that provision was introduced it would have been very difficult to secure agreement between, on the one side, the so-called "territorialist" States who wanted the most comprehensive possible rights in the economic zone, and, on the other, the maritime States who saw the economic zone as representing a limitation upon the high seas rights that they would otherwise enjoy. Consequently, what may look to us like a relatively meaningless proposition played an important part in achieving success in the negotiations. Even though almost every significant expression which the Article employs is open to criticism on account of its lack of precision, the fact is that without that Article the Conference might never have got past a crucial point in the negotiations.

There is a further and vitally important advantage in the introduction into a treaty text of this kind of provision. Coupled with a compulsory dispute settlement provision, it enables the parties to have recourse to a third party for the purpose of filling, in a specific context, the gap in respect of which they had, at the time of negotiation, found themselves unable to formulate a precise guiding rule.

b. *Customary international law*

Now, having mentioned some of the treaty contexts in which recourse has been had to equity, it is possible to move on to the customary international law provenance of some of the situations in which equity has been applied.

Here, one important class of material is to be found in judicial decisions – cases in which tribunals have had recourse to equity not because the parties expressly so requested but because the tribunal has found that the law applicable to the subject matter of the case itself prescribes a solution in terms of equity or equitable principles.

There appear to be two principal classes of cases in which this development is reflected: one consists of continental shelf delimitation cases; the other of cases relating to the determination of compensation for the taking by States of foreign-owned property.

i. *Continental shelf delimitation cases*

The first illustration of this process is provided by the decisions of the ICJ in the *North Sea Continental Shelf Cases*.[16] The seminal character of these cases requires that close scrutiny should be given to the manner in which the Court determined that it was entitled to apply equitable principles and the manner in which it did so.

These cases, it will be recalled, were ones in which the Court, by agreement between the parties, was asked to decide what principles and rules of international law were applicable to the delimitation of the continental shelf between them. The Court determined that there were two controlling "basic legal notions": one was that delimitation must be the object of agreement between the States concerned; the other was that such agreement must be arrived at in accordance with basic equitable principles.

How did the Court reach the view that it was entitled to apply "equitable principles"? It appears that the source of the Court's approach is a single sentence in a report of a committee of experts nominated by the International Law Commission in 1953 to provide the Commission with technical assistance in formulating rules relating to the delimitation of the territorial sea and continental shelf. This committee of experts, which consisted not of lawyers but of cartographers, suggested to the ILC that the strict application of the concept of equidistance (which is an exact way of approaching delimitation and which had been thought of as being

---

[16] (1969). *ICJ Reports 1969*, 3, 41 *ILR* 29.

a rule that would be certain and predictable in operation)[17] might in certain circumstances give rise to an inequitable solution.[18] They did not elaborate on what they meant by inequitable. Neither did the ILC. Nor did the Geneva Conference on the Law of the Sea in 1958. Nonetheless, in 1969, the International Court felt itself able to identify the concept of equity as being a rule of customary international law to be applied to the delimitation of adjacent and opposite continental shelves though it never specifically identified the positive basis on which its recourse to equity was justified; and to this concept the Court attached controlling importance.[19]

The obscurity which the Court thus introduced into the "law" relating to delimitation was increased by some lack of internal cogency in the judgment. The Court was dealing with the problem of the delimitation of the continental shelf between Germany, Holland and Denmark. Denmark and Holland had argued that the rule to be applied in this situation was one of equidistance. Germany had denied that the rule of equidistance formed part of customary international law. The Court, in rejecting the Danish and Dutch arguments, said, by way of criticism of the application of the equidistance principle, that "in certain geographical circumstances ... the equidistance method ... leads unquestionably to inequity".[20] The Court pointed out that the slightest irregularity in the coastline is magnified by the application of the principle of equidistance. It then continued: "Thus, it has been seen in the

---

[17] See, generally, Weil, *The Law of Maritime Delimitation – Reflections* (1989).
[18] *ICJ Reports 1969*, 34, 41 *ILR* 64.
[19] On 16 May 1978 Sir Gerald Fitzmaurice kindly sent the author some observations on the paper published under the title "Equity, Evasion, Equivocation and Evolution in International Law" in *Proceedings and Committee Reports of the American Branch of the International Law Association, 1977-1978*, 33, on part of which this chapter has drawn. Sir Gerald said of the critical comments there made on the *North Sea Continental Shelf Cases* and the *Anglo-French Continental Shelf Case* (and which reappear here): "Your strictures ... on the failure of the ICJ *et al.* to state explicity what principles of equity they were applying, and whence derived, are justified up to a point but not wholly ... for the reasons that you give yourself ... In addition, where (as in all the cases you mention) the Tribunal is precluded by its Statute or terms of reference from deciding *ex aequo et bono*, but is in fact doing just that, it cannot avow it, and has to take refuge in silence. Additionally, principles of equity *praeter legem* are often inherently difficult to define precisely." (Sir Gerald's emphasis) (Letter on file.)
[20] *ICJ Reports 1969*, 49, 41 *ILR* 78.

case of concave or convex coastlines that if the equidistance method is employed, then the greater the irregularity and the further from the coastline the area to be delimited, the more unreasonable are the results produced".[21] Now comes the important sentence: "So great an exaggeration of the consequences of a natural geographical feature must be remedied or compensated for as far as possible, being of itself creative of inequity".[22]

The critical reader must pause at this point and ask himself: what is the inequity thus created? The "exaggeration" is only inequitable if one assumes that, in general, territory is distributed amongst States in an equitable manner, which it is clearly not. The Court appears to have sensed this difficulty and so a few lines later it continued as follows: "There can never be any question of completely refashioning nature, and equity does not require that a State without access to the sea should be allotted an area of continental shelf, any more than there could be a question of rendering the situation of a State with an extensive coastline similar to that of a State with a restricted coastline. Equality is to be reckoned within the same plane, and it is not such natural inequalities as these that equity could remedy." But where is the source of the rule thus asserted that equality,[23] and with it equity, must be reckoned within the same plane? The Court provided no reasoned explanation of that proposition.[24] Later the Court

---

[21] *Id.*
[22] *Id.*
[23] *Id.*
[24] Sir Gerald Fitzmaurice (see n. 19 above) commented on this point as follows:
"I think the I.C.J. in the *North Sea* case thought that the reasons for this principle were too obvious to need explicit statement. You can only usefully compare the relative weight or thrust of things that belong broadly to the same class or category. There are innumerable examples of this in everyday life. Boxing affords as good an example as any. Boxers are only adjudged – indeed can only compete at all – within their own respective weight-categories, from 'fly', 'bantam', 'feather' etc. up to heavy weight. Moreover the difference between several of these weights is only a matter of a few pounds. Other things being equal a 15" gun battleship *must* outclass a 6" gun cruiser. You can only compare cruiser with cruiser. The same notion underlies all handicapping (golf, horse-racing, etc.), and similarly, graduated tax rates. You may prefer gothic architecture as a category to classical; but it is profitless to compare Chartres, as an individual building, with the Parthenon. So the I.C.J. thought that in delineating the

elaborated the concept of equity with factors such as these: the general configuration of the coasts, the physical and geological structure and resources of the continental shelf, and a reasonable degree of proportionality between a continental shelf and the length of a coast.[25] In so doing, the Court was performing a distinctly legislative role – albeit in terms that did not in themselves give very clear guidance as to the outcome of their cumulative application. Moreover, it was clearly making policy decisions in that it was tacitly excluding from consideration broader factors of equity such as the relative size of the parties, the wealth of their populations, or the dependence of each upon access to natural resources within its own territory.[26]

We can examine the award of the arbitral tribunal in the *Anglo-French Continental Shelf Case* in the same way. Here the tribunal decided that its task was to apply equity in two contexts. One was in relation to the drawing of a line between the continental shelf adhering to the Channel Islands and the continental shelf adhering to the adjacent French mainland; the second was in drawing a line between the French and British continental shelves in the western approaches. The Tribunal did in fact identify a number of factors which in its judgment affected the equities. It is to be noted that these factors are not identical with those which were identified in the *North Sea Continental Shelf Cases* and in some

---

maritime boundaries between the adjacent coastlines of two countries you had to take account of the respective characters of these coastlines. You could not "re-fashion nature" by, for instance, treating a broken, indented, coast as you would a smooth, continuous one, or vice-versa. But where both coastlines were, say, smooth and continuous, and of about the same length, you could then, as a matter of equity, seek to eliminate incidental differences that would lead to the allocation of quite disproportionately different areas of sea-bed. I admit that there may be considerable difficulty in the application of such a notion to particular situations; but as a principle I would not have thought it needed much explaining or justifying."

[25] *ICJ Reports 1969*, 50-52.
[26] Sir Gerald Fitzmaurice (see n. 19 above) commented on this point as follows:

"... the Court – (so far as it was itself concerned, – it might be different in a private negotiation between the parties) – *was* purporting tacitly to exclude such factors as those you mention, these being mainly of a different *order* from those it did include, i.e. factors mainly of a political and economic character, rather than of a geographical, structural or littoral (coastal) character. Of course you can argue as to whether the Court got its categories right, but that was the basis of it, I think."

important respects go wider than those factors. In the Channel Islands section, which was a part that was being dealt with by reference to customary international law, the Court made the following points. Where opposite coastlines are approximately equal in relation to the disputed continental shelf the areas of continental shelf should be broadly equal or broadly comparable.[27] The tribunal excluded the political status of the Channel Islands as a factor affecting the situation.[28] However, it mentioned the size and importance of the islands and said that they might properly be taken into account in balancing the equities.[29] It referred to the extent of the territorial sea of the Channel Islands.[30] It spoke of the navigational, defence and security interests of the two countries, saying that they could not be decisive and commenting that in any event France had a predominant interest in the continental shelf in the southern part of the Channel.[31] It observed that the principle of natural prolongation is not absolute.[32] It said that the equality of States is not an element of equity.[33] It spoke of the possibility of redressing inequities by the use of available space; in other words, if something was taken away from one country in a particular area it would be relevant that that country might be able to balance what it had lost in that area by the possibility of extending its claim in another.[34]

And having spoken of those various factors, it then reached the following conclusion as regards delimitation involving the Channel Islands. First, it drew a median line between France and England in approximately mid-Channel.[35] Then it gave the Channel Islands themselves an enclave of continental shelf.[36] Somewhat surprisingly, this enclave was limited to a width of 12

---

[27] Award, para. 182. The Award is printed in 54 *ILR* 6.
[28] *Ibid.*, para. 186.
[29] *Ibid.*, para. 187.
[30] *Id.*
[31] *Ibid.*, para. 188.
[32] *Ibid.*, paras. 190-194.
[33] *Ibid.*, para. 195.
[34] *Ibid.*, para. 200.
[35] *Ibid.*, para. 201.
[36] *Ibid.*, para. 202.

MODES OF INTRODUCING EQUITY

miles – a width to which the Channel Islands would in any event have been entitled if the United Kingdom had used the "potentiality" (to use the word of the Court)[37] to claim 12 miles of territorial sea for them. Thus, after all the equitable factors had been considered, the Channel Islands were given no more continental shelf than they would have had if Great Britain had claimed for them a 12-mile territorial sea.[38]

Now, the important point, the point to which this section relates, is that no explanation was given as to how the various factors mentioned by the tribunal actually led it to the conclusion that 12 miles, not 6, nor 18 or more, was the appropriate width of continental shelf to attribute to the Channel Islands.[39]

The same sort of problem arose in the western sector. There the Court, for reasons which are not material here, was applying not customary international law but Article 6 of the 1958 Geneva Convention on the Continental Shelf. However, the principle to be applied was the same – the principle of equity.[40] And there the Court was faced by the following situation: England projects to the west in the form of the Cornish Peninsula, and 21 miles beyond the Cornish Peninsula lie the Scilly Islands. France projects to the west in the form of Brittany; and 10 miles to the northwest of the tip of Brittany lies the island of Ushant.

The Court decided that the Scilly Islands should not be given full weight as an element in the determination of the boundary of the continental shelf, but only half weight.[41] It made no reference at all

---

[37] *Ibid.*, para. 187.
[38] Sir Gerald Fitzmaurice (see n. 19 above) commented on this point as follows:
"I do agree this illustrates very well the difficulty of *applying* equitable principles, however impeccable in themselves, to a given situation. But in my view the Anglo-French Tribunal in the Channel case, while purporting to apply equity *intra* or *secundum legem*, was really – in the conclusions it reached about the Channel Islands Group and the Scilly Isles – acting *ex aequo et bono*, or on the extreme outer edge of *praeter legem*. However, this could not be avowed because the Tribunal's terms of reference enjoined a decision on a legal basis, – which, of course, did not exclude principles of equity *according to law*; but, since no such principles led to the conclusions reached concerning these groups, the Tribunal had to remain silent as to the basis of its action."
[39] Unless it is to be found in the Award, paras. 198-202.
[40] *Ibid.*, para. 238.
[41] *Ibid.*, paras. 248-251.

to the position of Ushant, and treated Ushant as having full weight. No explanation was given of either conclusion. And yet both conclusions reflected the application by the Court of principles of equity. In short, the Tribunal, in exercising its equitable discretion, has not shared with anyone else the precise considerations that led to its specific conclusions.

ii. *Compensation cases*

Matters are no better in the other category of case in which resort has been had to equity, namely, those involving the quantum of compensation to be paid by a State for the taking of the property of an alien. There have been at least three important cases in the Iran-US Claims Tribunal in which the relevant Chamber has referred to "equity" in this connection and in a manner indicative of a disinclination to grapple specifically with the positive legal requirements applicable to the situation. These were laid down in the 1955 Treaty of Amity between Iran and the US, of which Article IV(2) prescribed that property of the nationals of the two countries "shall not be taken ... without the prompt payment of just compensation". Content was then immediately given to this otherwise vague phrase by the words next following: "Such compensation shall be in an effectively realizable form and shall represent the full equivalent of the property taken".

It is important, in considering the cases in which this provision has been applied, to bear in mind the distinction between two words: valuation and compensation. "Valuation" describes the process of determining the economic worth of an object. "Compensation" refers to one of a number of possible processes that may follow a valuation. Thus valuation must take place as the first step towards an award of compensation upon a compulsory taking. But a valuation of property must also be made for the purpose, say, of levying a capital gains tax or for determining the price which a prospective purchaser of the property may wish to pay. In short, valuation is an objective process carried out by reference to certain accountancy techniques. No doubt it may involve the exercise of discretion by a valuer – but the elements of discretion are always strictly related to the character of the item being valued. The determination of compensation, on the other hand, can in theory be influenced by any number of external factors, such as the amount available to pay compensation, the respective positions of the owner and the expropriator, or the extent to which the owner has hitherto benefitted from the property in question. There is no absolute requirement that value and compensation should be equal. Their relationship will depend entirely upon the applicable legal rule – for example, that in the particular case, the owner shall receive compensation amounting to only 10% of the value or, in another situation, that the owner shall receive full value.

Or to put the point in a slightly different way – one can use "equitable" as an adjective qualifying compensation – because that is a word with a possibly variable content. One cannot use "equitable" as an adjective to qualify value, because that is a result that can only have meaning if objectively determined.

With these points in mind, we can now turn to three cases in which the Iran-US Claims Tribunal appears to have misapplied equitable concepts.

The first case was that of *Starrett Housing* v. *Iran*,[42] a claim arising out of the premature termination of a contract for the construction of a major housing project in Iran and the expropriation of the American-owned interest in the venture. The Chamber appointed an expert to value the enterprise and instructed him to apply the accounting method known as the "discounted cash flow" or "DCF" method in order to find the amount of "the full equivalent of the property taken". On that basis he produced a figure of 377 million Rials. But although the decision asserts that "the Tribunal largely accepts the positions of the Expert", it found that in three respects "a hypothetical reasonable businessman" (whose reasoning, if any, in such circumstances was never articulated) would have made different calculations. As a result, the Tribunal reduced the Expert's determination of the value by some 92.83 per cent, to no

---

[42] 4 *Iran-US CTR* 122 and 16 *Iran-US CTR* 112.

more than 27 million Rials. The Tribunal did this on the basis of an alleged principle "that when the circumstances militate against calculation of a precise figure, the Tribunal is obliged to exercise its discretion to 'determine equitably' the amount involved".[43]

Where did this principle, with its removal of the determination of value from the realm of the rationally justifiable to that of unspecified subjective discretion, come from?[44] The Tribunal is directed by Article V of the Claims Settlement Declaration to "decide all cases on the basis of respect for law, applying such ... principles ... of international law as the Tribunal determines to be applicable".[45] There is nothing there about the substitution of equity for law. Nor, on close scrutiny, is there anything in the four precedents cited by the Tribunal that supports its approach. In the first case referred to by the Tribunal it was obliged to resort to an "equitable determination" because the Claimant had produced only general testimony which was unsatisfactory for the precise computation of damages. This "equitable determination" was therefore not in competition with objectively verifiable figures.[46] In the second case, the Tribunal did not refer to "equitable determination" but after a careful consideration of the components of valuation made "a global assessment" which has nothing to do with the matter in hand.[47] In the third case, the Tribunal did no more than follow the first case in a situation where

---

[43] 16 *Iran-US CTR*, at 221.
[44] This approach may be contrasted with that of the ICSID Tribunal in *Amco Asia Corporation and others* v. *The Republic of Indonesia* (*Resubmitted Case*), award of 31 May 1990 (unpublished). (Prof. R. Higgins, QC (Chairman, UK), the Hon. Marc Lalonde, PC, QC (Canada) and Mr Per Magid (Denmark)). In introducing its treatment of valuation, it said:
"It is the Tribunal's intention that its decisions on the method of valuation, and its reasons therefore, should be fully transparent" (Award, para. 188).
At para. 199 the Tribunal also said:
"... the Tribunal calls attention to the fact that it is not a mechanistic device. The method itself relies on the application of assumptions which are necessarily judgmental. The DCF method is at once a flexible tool, that allows for the application of factors and elements judged as relevant. At the same time it allows for the application of these judgmental elements to be articulated."
[45] Text in 1 *Iran-US CTR* 9.
[46] *Economy Forms Corp.* v. *Islamic Republic of Iran* (1983), 3 *Iran-US CTR* 42, 52.
[47] *Sola Tiles, Inc.* v. *Islamic Republic of Iran* (1987), 14 *Iran-US CTR* 223, 242.

the Claimant had failed to provide necessary documentary evidence.[48] And in the fourth case, there was no reference to an "equitable determination", only a reference to "fair market value", which is something else entirely.[49] This citation of authority is impressive only because it is so unpersuasive.

The tendency thus demonstrated to bring the concept of equity into the assessment of compensation was carried even further in another case before the same Tribunal, the *Amoco International Finance Corporation* case.[50] In discussing the various methods of valuation that might be employed, the Chamber said: "The choice between all the available methods must rather be made in view of the purpose to be attained, in order to avoid arbitrary results and to arrive at an *equitable compensation* in conformity with the applicable legal standards. The use of several methods, when possible, is also commendable."[51]

This passage calls for close scrutiny. One must note that the valuation exercise is here described by reference to two concepts. Neither of them had previously been mentioned in the case. They are (1) the avoidance of arbitrary results and (2) the attainment of equitable compensation. To the first concept, no one could take exception. But if the avoidance of arbitrary results is an objective which one can wholeheartedly pursue, the second concept, the suggestion that the positive goal is the attainment of "equitable compensation", is something to which one is obliged to take exception. It is not that anyone seeks "inequitable" compensation; it is that the whole concept of equity is out of place when it comes to the application of a specific legal formula like "the full equivalent of the property taken" as dictated by the 1955 Treaty. If the Parties to that Treaty had wished to use "equitable" as the standard of compensation they could have so provided. This would have

---

[48] *William J. Levitt* v. *Islamic Republic of Iran* (1987), 14 *Iran-US CTR* 191, 205.
[49] *Thomas Earl Payne* v. *Government of Islamic Republic of Iran* (1986), 12 *Iran-US CTR* 3, 15.
[50] 15 *Iran-US CTR* 189. The decision here was prepared by the Chairman of Chamber Three, the late Professor M. Virally.
[51] *Ibid.*, 256 (emphasis supplied).

meant that the Treaty provisions would have read thus: "Property shall not be taken without the prompt payment of just compensation. Such compensation shall be equitable compensation." But the Treaty does not say this, just as it does not say that the general international law standard shall be applied. The Treaty is quite specific and does not permit the erosion of the precise obligation to pay the "full equivalent" by the addition of it to a reference to the concept of equity. Even if equity does have a place in the assessment of compensation under customary international law, it is not the equivalent, or the replacement, of the Treaty provision establishing "the full equivalent of the property taken" as the standard of the compensation to be paid.

There are thus really two separate criticisms that may be levelled against the approach of the Chamber. First, in the part of the decision dealing with valuation (as opposed to the level of compensation), use is made of language relevant to the standard of compensation. The second is that the Chamber thereby displays its belief that equitable considerations are relevant to the process of valuation. The suggestion that the standard of *compensation* payable upon a lawful nationalization or expropriation is determined by reference to equity is one which, though one may not accept it as the standard presented by the relevant treaty, cannot be said to be conceptually out of order. But, to the extent that equity is given an additional and earlier role by applying it to the process of *valuation*, error creeps in.

The third pertinent case from the Iran-US Claims Tribunal is the decision of Chamber Two in the *Phillips* case[52] – which also involved the assessment of compensation for the taking of oil company interests. Here, at any rate, there appears some explanation for the presence of the reference to "equity", but it is not satisfactory. "The need for some adjustments is understandable, as the determination of value by a tribunal must take into account all relevant circumstances, including equitable

---

[52] *Phillips Petroleum Company Iran* v. *The Islamic Republic of Iran*, 29 June 1989, 21 *Iran-US CTR* 79. For the effect of the subsequent settlement agreement, see the statements of Judges Aldrich and Khalilian, *ibid.*, 293-301.

considerations."[53] To this sentence there is added – by way of citation of authority – a footnote referring to two paragraphs of the *Aminoil* Award.[54] The first reference contains the following statement: "It is well known that any estimate in money terms of amounts intended to express the value of an asset, of an undertaking, of a contract, or of services rendered, must take equitable principles into account".[55] The second reference contains no express mention of equity. It emphasizes the need to enquire into "all the circumstances" when determining the amount of an award of "appropriate" compensation.[56]

The second citation is clearly out of place in connection with the *Phillips* case since the exercise there was the determination not of "appropriate" compensation but of "the full equivalent" of the value of the asset taken – a rather different matter. As to the first citation, although two references are given – one to the *Corfu Channel Case*[57] and the other to the *North Sea Continental Shelf Cases*[58] – neither really appears to support the dictum. As a result the observation assumes the quality of an *ex cathedra* statement which, though possibly applicable in the *Aminoil* situation (a different case with different requirements), is scarcely appropriate for application to a "full equivalent" situation such as that in the *Phillips* case.

Attractive though the concept of equity may be in many situations, and perhaps as much beyond criticism as is mother love, it is not a concept that can be sprinkled like salt on every part of the law. There are many situations in which the law prescribes absolute rules. The limit of the exclusive economic zone is 200 miles; not 200 miles subject to equitable considerations. The duty to refrain from the use of poison gas is absolute – it is not qualified by reference to "equitable requirements". The treaty obligation that compensation be the "full equivalent" of property taken is also

---

[53] Para. 112, *ibid.*, 123.
[54] *Government of Kuwait* v. *American Independent Oil Company (Aminoil)*, 24 March 1982. (Reuter, President; Hamed Sultan and Sir Gerald Fitzmaurice.) 66 *ILR* 519.
[55] Para. 78, *ibid.*, 581.
[56] Para. 144, *ibid.*, 602.
[57] *ICJ Reports 1949*, 249, 16 *ILR* 342, 343.
[58] *ICJ Reports 1969*, 3, 47, 41 *ILR* 29, 76.

absolute – unless the treaty provides otherwise. It is, therefore, quite wrong to introduce the notion of "equity" into this last situation. If absolutes are to be qualified by "equity" or "equitable considerations", that qualification must be expressly stated. Otherwise its introduction will seriously weaken the legal effect of clear rules.[59]

2. *By reason of express request to decide* ex aequo et bono *or to formulate rules or recommendations*

It is now possible to pass briefly to the second main class of situations in which tribunals may come to apply equity or equitable principles. This is where tribunals are expressly given the power to formulate rules for, or make recommendations to the parties.[60]

---

[59] Mention may also be made, in the context of customary international law, of two further examples: (i) The so-called Helsinki Rules of 1966, dealing with the question of entitlement to water resources, drawn up by the International Law Association, provided that each basin State is entitled to "a reasonable and equitable share" in the common water resources (ILA, *Report of the Fifty-second Conference, Helsinki*, 1966, 484 *et seq.*) Some attempt was made to expand the concept of equity by the provision that what is "a reasonable and equitable share" is to be determined "in the light of all the relevant factors in each particular case". This was followed by an enumeration of such factors as geography, hydrology, climate, past utilization, economic and social needs of each State, the population dependent on the waters, the comparative cost of alternative means of satisfying those needs, the avoidance of waste and the practicability of compensation. (ii) The draft articles prepared by the ILC on State succession in respect of matters other than treaties provide, in the section on succession to property, when dealing with movable property in the case of separation of parts of a State or dissolution of a State, that property connected with the activity of the predecessor State in respect of the territory affected by the succession shall pass to the successor State. Other movable property of the predecessor State shall pass to the successor in equitable proportion. (See *Report of the International Law Commission on the work of its 28th session, 1976*, UN doc. A/31/10, 316-319. (Introductory comment to Section 2 of Part I of the draft.))

[60] In the *Sapphire* case (*Sapphire International Petroleums Ltd. v. National Iranian Oil Company* (1963), 35 *ILR* 135), the Arbitrator, Judge Pierre Cavin, took care to emphasize that, in finding that the law applicable to the contract in question was "the principles of law generally recognized by civilized nations", he had "no intention of deciding the case according to 'equity', like an *'amiable compositeur'*". (*Ibid.*, 175.) This may be contrasted with the award of Ripert and Panchaud in *Société Européenne d'Etudes et d'Entreprises v. People's Federal Republic of Yugoslavia* (1956), 24 *ILR* 761, in which, charged with the duty of deciding as *amiables compositeurs*, the arbitrators found, *inter alia*, that "it is consistent with equity that the payment, having been delayed for a number of years, should correspond to the actual value of that by which the Yugoslav Government benefited". (*Ibid.*, 765.)

Thus, while the case of the *Free Zones of Upper Gex and Savoy*[61] is frequently mentioned as the occasion when the parties reached agreement to ask the Court for a decision *ex aequo et bono*, but did so too late, it is not often recalled that subsequent to the judgment the two parties, with the assistance of three experts whom they jointly selected, pursued negotiations towards a settlement. Not all the outstanding questions were successfully resolved in this way and the experts were then required to complete the settlement on their own. This they did by an arbitral award establishing with binding force a set of regulations controlling the import into Switzerland of products of the Free Zones.[62]

Mention may also be made of the revision by arbitral process after the First World War of concessions relating to such matters as railways.[63] By way of example of the operation of the process, some details of the proceedings in the *Sopron-Köszeg* case may be given.[64] The case stemmed from Article 320 of the Treaty of St Germain:

With the object of ensuring regular utilisation of the railroads of the former Austro-Hungarian Monarchy owned by private companies which, as a result of the stipulations of the present Treaty, will be situated in the territory of several States, the administrative and technical reorganization of the said lines shall be regulated in each

---

[61] PCIJ, Ser. A/B, No. 46, 96.

[62] PCIJ, Ser. E, No. 10, 106. The terms of reference of the Commission, as recorded by themselves, were "to regulate in a manner more appropriate to the economic conditions of the present day the terms of exchange of goods between the regions in question". (*Ibid.*, 108.) A comparable case, where the arbitrator was accorded a legislative function, is that part of the *Tacna-Arica* arbitration (1925) in which the arbitrator was empowered, in case he should decide that a plebiscite was to be held in the disputed area, "to determine the conditions thereof". Finding that a plebiscite should be held, the arbitrator said:

"The conditions of the plebiscite should be such as will be plain and practical and work substantial justice between the Parties in the present circumstances. They have also been framed in the light of the proposals made and views expressed by the Parties respectively in the course of their negotiations, and the Arbitrator has not failed to consider whatever historical precedents may be deemed to be of value." (2 *UNRIAA* 923, 944; 3 *ILR* 357.)

[63] *Sopron-Köszeg Local Railway Company v. Austria*, 24 *AJIL* 164 (1930), 5 *ILR* 57; *Re Zeltweg-Wolfsberg and Unterdrauburg-Woellan Railways*, 7 *ILR* 429; *Barcs-Pakrac Railway Co. v. Yugoslavia*, 29 *AJIL* 523 (1935), 7 *ILR* 424. See also Shawcross in 102 *Hague Recueil* (1961-I), 357-358.

[64] The full report is in *LNOJ*, Oct. 1928, 1609 *et seq.*

instance by an agreement between the owning company and the States territorially concerned.

Any differences on which agreement is not reached, including questions relating to the interpretation of contracts concerning the expropriation of the lines shall be submitted to arbitrators designated by the Council of the League of Nations.

The Sopron-Köszeg Local Railway Company operated a line across the frontier between Austria and Hungary. It was able to negotiate satisfactory terms with the Hungarian Government, but not with the Austrian Government. Accordingly, in 1927, it applied to the Council of the League for the appointment of arbitrators pursuant to the Treaty.[65]

The resolution appointing the arbitrators did no more to define their functions than indicate that they were "to settle the disputes which stand in the way of agreement between the company and the States territorially concerned". However, the arbitrators set out their own conception of their function in a passage of the Award where they clearly contemplated that their function extended beyond a mere finding of the respective rights of the parties:

> Holding that the arbitrators are required, by the terms of Articles 304 of the Treaty of Trianon and 320 of the Treaty of St Germain, to effect, in their award, a final and general settlement of the questions raised in the Company's request to the Council of the League of Nations, and that they should, with that end in view:
> First, define the Company's rights in relation to the Austrian State from 5 January 1922 up to the date of the present decision, and for the future, its rights in relation to the two States territorially concerned;
> Secondly, lay the foundation of the administrative and technical reorganization of the Sopron-Köszeg railway, bearing in mind their decisions on the first point.[66]
>
> Considering that, whilst the pre-war contracts between the concession-granting state and the concession-holding company should be respected in their main lines, they could not be enforced literally

---

[65] The Council appointed M. Guerrero (El Salvador), M. Kalff (Netherlands) and M. R. Mayer (France).
[66] *LNOJ*, Sep. 1929, 1360.

and in full without disregarding the position brought about by the 1914-1918 war and its political and economic consequences, the treaties of peace and, in particular, Articles 304 of the Treaty of Trianon and 320 of the Treaty of Saint Germain, or without disregarding the extent of the powers of the arbitrators whose intervention is contemplated in the aforesaid clauses; that the very existence of these peace treaty provisions shows the high contracting parties to have foreseen that special difficulties would hamper the reorganization of the railways of the former Austro-Hungarian Monarchy; that, for the solution thereof, they contemplated fresh agreements to be concluded between the concession holders and the states territorially concerned, whereby the position under previous contracts was to be brought into harmony not only with the new political circumstances but also with the economic situation created by the war and the break-up of the Dual Monarchy; that, failing agreement, the treaties provided for arbitration, and this could not be confined to the enforcement of the old contract clauses, which remain valid as to their principle but cannot be equitably enforced without extensive modifications...[67]

From this passage it is evident that the Tribunal saw its task as being not only one of determining rights but also of laying down a new regime to reflect equitably the changed conditions arising out of the new political circumstances and economic conditions; and the Tribunal clearly thought of this as being, in effect, an application of equity.

The Award contains little reference to the procedure followed. It mentions the documents laid before it, the proceedings of the Council relating to the appointment of the Tribunal, an interlocutory decision regarding costs and concludes with a statement that it had heard "the observations" of the representatives of the parties.[68]

The basic considerations controlling the approach of the Tribunal were expressed as follows:

> The arbitrators should...take account both of the legitimate interests

---

[67] *Ibid.*, 1361-2.
[68] *Id.*

involved in the public utility undertaking concerned and of the purpose set before them by the Treaties of Peace, which is to restore the regular operation of the railways of the former Austro-Hungarian Monarchy in the higher interests of the facility and freedom of international communication.[69]

In approaching the question regarding the administrative and technical reorganization of the railway, the arbitrators opened the discussion by "holding" that "in order to achieve the purpose thus defined, the whole line must, obviously for technical reasons, be brought under the control of one and the same administration". The arbitrators expressed themselves as being much helped by the existence of a Protocol of 1922 concluded between the Austrian and Hungarian Governments "which furnished internationally accepted technical grounds for the operation of the whole line by the Austrian railways".[70] The reasoning leading to their conclusion (that a series of transactions should lead to the vesting of the railway in the Austrian Government) did not go beyond this.

When dealing with the determination of the amounts to be paid to the Company, the arbitrators several times described their assessments as "equitable". In fixing the amount of capital to be repaid, the tribunal treated as relevant the consideration that the shareholders must have foreseen the prospect of loss as well as of profit and concluded therefore that the governments and the company should share the losses due to the war and its economic consequences.[71] In working this out in greater detail, the arbitrators took account of the reduced railway traffic following upon the altered frontier and the extensive investment which the Austrian Government had had to make in the line since beginning to run it in the period prior to the award. They also noted that as part of the Company's share capital had been subscribed by the Hungarian Government this should be regarded as a "free grant" for the construction of the line upon which no return or

[69] *Id.*
[70] *Id.*
[71] *Id.*

redemption should be calculated. No reasons were given for this conclusion.

When eventually fixing the final capital amount to be paid for the acquisition of the railway this was done "equitably" as a lump sum expressed in gold francs. No breakdown of the figure was given. In prescribing that the amount should be paid in 65 annual instalments at 3 1/2% annual interest, the arbitrators gave no further explanations and clearly did not contemplate that any significant change in interest rates would occur. As to the amount of compensation due for the period from 1922 to 1929, when the Company had received no payments for the use of the line by the Austrian Government, the arbitrators again equitably fixed the sum at 600,000 gold francs. In spreading the payment of this over 65 years the arbitrators had regard to financial considerations advanced by the Austrian Government, but did not say what they were or why they led specifically to that conclusion.

In similar vein, one may also refer to the two very interesting awards, in the period after the Second World War, of Mr von Steyern and Mr Eugene Black respectively relating to the revision of Japanese external loans.[72] In the first of these the arbitrator was requested to advise on the manner in which, following the events of the war and the associated depreciation of currency, the Japanese Government should settle its obligations under a loan raised by it in 1910. After reaching certain legal conclusions about the interpretation of the currency clause, the arbitrator went on to say:

> However, a settlement established on such basis could no longer be described as equitable ... Pressing considerations of equity require ... that the damage to the foreign bondholders should be reduced to some extent in such a way as to compensate them without too much parsimony for the loss incurred, not as a result of their fault, but as a result of the long interruption in the service of the loan and as a consequence of the very serious fall in the value of the French and

---

[72] *Re Imperial Japanese Government 4% Loan of 1910* (1955), 29 *ILR* 4, (von Steyern, conciliator); *Re City of Tokyo 5% Loan of 1912* (1960), 29 *ILR* 11, (Black, conciliator).

Japanese currency. In these circumstances, there remains no other solution than a revalorization worked out on a basis which would appear reasonable.

The arbitrator then made certain proposals amounting, in his view, to a "practicable and equitable solution".[73]

The second award related to a comparable situation arising out of a different loan raised by Japan. The President of the World Bank, acting as conciliator, said that his task was not a judicial one but that of giving a fair and practical opinion for the resumption of the payment of principal and interest on an equitable basis. Accordingly, he drew up a Plan to this end which, it is understood, was accepted and implemented by the parties.[74]

Perhaps the most recent illustration of this practice is provided by the Report and Recommendations of the Conciliation Commission appointed to establish a dividing line for the shelf area between Iceland and Jan Mayen Island.[75] A Conciliation Commission is, of its very nature, not intended to be a body that makes recommendations on the basis of strict law and so the work of this Commission stands as a good illustration of a deliberately innovative approach. The Agreement establishing the Commission stipulated that in preparing its recommendations "the Commission shall take into account Iceland's strong economic interests in these sea areas, the existing geographical and geological factors and other special circumstances".

The Commission itself said that it followed from its mandate that it should not act as a court of law. "Its function is to make recommendations to the two governments which ... will lead to acceptable and equitable solutions of the problems involved." The

---

[73] 29 *ILR* 9-10. On 31 May 1955 the Japanese Government issued a press release stating that it was its policy to accept the opinion of Mr von Steyern. On the same day the Association Nationale des Porteurs Français de Valeurs Mobilières announced that it would examine with its advisers the situation resulting from the proposal. (Letters on file from the General Counsel of the International Monetary Fund, 14 March 1978, and from the above-mentioned Association, 26 April 1978.)
[74] 29 *ILR* 15-20. Letter on file from the Vice-President and General Counsel of the World Bank, 14 April 1978.
[75] 62 *ILR* 108.

essence of the Commission's recommendations was that, instead of a demarcation line, there should be a joint development arrangement for that part of the area in which there was a significant prospect of hydrocarbon development.

There are also a number of treaties containing provisions for what amounts, in effect, to third party determinations of an equitable nature. Thus, the International Air Services Transit Agreement 1944[76] contains in Article II(1) a provision enabling one contracting State which considers that the action of another contracting State under the Agreement is causing the first "injustice or hardship" to request the Council to examine the situation and make appropriate findings and recommendations. As the ICJ recognized in its Advisory Opinion on the *Appeal relating to the Jurisdiction of the ICAO Council*,[77] the Council is here being empowered to act where a party "although acting within its legal rights under the Treaties, has nevertheless caused injustice or hardship to another party – a case not of illegal action ... but of action lawful, yet prejudicial" and to base its findings and recommendations "on considerations of equity and expediency such as would not constitute suitable material for appeal to a court of law".[78]

The Euratom Treaty contemplates that in certain circumstances holders of patents relating to inventions directly connected with nuclear research or the development of nuclear energy may be obliged to grant to the Community or to persons or undertakings non-exclusive licences to use those patents.[79] If amicable agreement cannot be reached, these licences "may be granted by arbitration".[80] For this purpose Article 18 established a special Arbitration Committee. If, when a matter is referred to it, the Committee finds that the conditions for a grant, as prescribed in Article 17, are satisfied "it shall give a reasoned decision containing a grant of the licence to the applicant and laying down the terms of

---

[76] See above, Ch. VI, n. 20.
[77] *ICJ Reports 1972*, 46.
[78] *Ibid.*, 58-59.
[79] See Euratom Treaty, Art. 17-23.
[80] Art. 17(1).

the licence and the remuneration therefor".[81] It would thus appear that the functions of the Arbitration Committee fall into two parts. First, the Committee is bound to perform the essentially legal function of determining whether the conditions prescribed in Article 17 are satisfied. Second, however, the Committee has to lay down the terms of the licence and the relevant remuneration. As the Treaty gives no guidance regarding the content of the licences or the amount of remuneration, it seems that the Arbitration Committee has been vested with a discretionary power analogous to a right to decide "equitably" or "fairly and reasonably". It is, in effect, constructing law for the parties.

A comparable "legislative" function is also envisaged by the artibration tribunal foreseen in the Agreement concerning International Arrangements relating to Polymetallic Nodules of the Deep Sea Bed, 1982.[82] Paragraph 9 of the Agreement provides that if a conflict, for example about overlapping areas, arises it shall, if not otherwise settled, be submitted to arbitration. Tacitly recognizing that there is no established law on the subject, the parties prescribed certain "Principles of Resolution of Conflicts" as follows:

1. In determining the issue as to which applicant involved in a conflict shall be awarded all or part of each area in conflict, the arbitral tribunal shall find a solution which is fair and equitable, having regard, with respect to each applicant involved in the conflict, to the following factors:
 (a) The continuity and extent of activities relevant to each area in conflict and the application area of which it is a part;
 (b) the date on which each applicant involved in the conflict or predecessor in interest or component organization thereof commenced activities at sea in the application area;
 (c) the financial cost of activities relevant to each area in conflict and to the application area of which it is a part, measured in constant terms;
 (d) the time when activities were carried out, and the quality of activities; and

---

[81] Art. 20.
[82] UK Treaty Series, No. 96 (1982), Cmnd. 8685.

PROCEDURAL ASPECTS OF APPLYING EQUITY   145

(e) such additional factors as the arbitral tribunal determines to be relevant, but excluding a consideration of the future plans of work of the applicants involved in the conflict. ...

C. PROCEDURAL ASPECTS OF THE APPLICATION OF EQUITY

An attempt can now be made to relate this examination of the application or applicability of equity in international law more closely to the procedural aspects of the administration of international justice. What has so far been described is an area of judicial, arbitral or conciliatory activity in which the tribunal is required, either by the content of the law or by the mandate of the parties, to exercise a substantial discretion – to reconcile divergent interests of coastal and other States within the economic zone, to decide whether a continental shelf boundary line shall be, say, 18 instead of 12 miles on one side or the other of an equidistance line, to determine whether compensation should be equal to or less than the objective value of property taken or to determine what rules should govern a customs regime at a border or the joint development of an oil field. In each of these situations the tribunal is being required to perform a role which is in substance legislative. It is not finding and applying law; it is deliberately constructing it for the parties in that case.

Some may say that these are merely examples of something that is different in degree, perhaps, but not different in kind to what courts are doing every day in every land. They will assert that there is no such thing as a court that does not "make" law since no rule of law is ever so completely expressed that it can perfectly cover every situation. The judge must always elaborate the rule to fit the case.

The truth of such generalities cannot be denied, but it is on the acknowledgment of the difference of degree, if not of kind, between the two processes that we should concentrate our attention. Is the nature of the decisions that the international judge is called upon to make in these "equitable" situations one that we may assimilate entirely to those of the national judge in applying the principles of the *Code Civil* to a problem of contract, in approving a variation of a trust or even in dealing with the winding up of a company? The answer, it may be suggested, is No – principally because the discretion that the international judge is exercising in the situations of the kind here described is larger in scale and in impact; and the range of factors that he may have to take into account is wider and more complex.

In these circumstances, we are bound to ask about the adequacy of the procedures that operate in cases where international tribunals have to exercise wide subjective discretions.

The content of the adversary procedure in international litigation is well established. We are accustomed to the idea of the parties presenting written and oral pleadings and of the tribunal subsequently withdrawing into isolation for the purpose of considering the arguments before it. But in cases where considerations of equity or equitable principles are relevant, and particularly where they have been introduced by one party in opposition to the views of the other, there is a possibility, if not a likelihood, that they may not have been sufficiently developed in the course of the pleadings. Thus, in the *North Sea Continental Shelf Cases*, Germany was vigorous in introducing arguments of equity because it was trying to establish what it called an equitable apportionment of the North Sea continental shelf. But Denmark and the Netherlands, which sought to stand upon the strictly legal concept of equidistance, were in the difficulty that, if they had introduced an argument relating to equity, this would have appeared to be inconsistent with their contention that the legal rule of equidistance was alone applicable. The only arguments about equity that the Netherlands and Denmark addressed to the Court were ones which related, not to delimitation as such, but to the specific German argument about equitable apportionment. And so it was that, when the Court came to consider the whole concept of equity as an element in delimitation, it did not have the benefit of argument by Denmark and the Netherlands in response to the German equitable contentions, nor had either side an opportunity to comment on the novel approach to equity that the Court generated *proprio motu*.

The same point also appears to be true of the *Anglo-French*

Continental Shelf arbitration. No argument appears to have been addressed to the Court on such questions as the appropriate width of continental shelf to be attached to the Channel Islands or the weight to be given to the Scilly Islands in comparison with that to be accorded to Ushant. Likewise, in the Iran-US Claims Tribunal cases to which reference has been made the claimant never had an opportunity to express its views on the equitable reduction of its claims.

As already suggested, the problem is especially acute where one party relies upon equity and the other opposes it. It must be appreciated that whether we are discussing a decision *ex aequo et bono* (in traditional terms, a decision completely outside the law) or whether we are considering equity in the sense of "equity within the law", we are talking about situations in which the court is being asked to apply a subjective or discretionary element. In situations in which the court is not applying the law but is creating it for the parties, it is essential that the court should have enough knowledge adequately to perform this task. Such knowledge must include a sufficient awareness of the views of the parties on the solutions which the court is considering or is likely to consider. There is, therefore, a real need for debate between the parties and the court. At the very least, the court should not decide such a case by reference to points which have not been precisely argued and elaborated before it. And, better still, it should go through a process of discussing such points in detail with the parties. This approach suggests that there is a strong case for the introduction in this kind of situation of a two-stage procedure – one which involves not only the traditional exchanges of written and oral pleadings but also a preliminary assessment by the court of the main elements of the case which, in its judgment, are going to affect its decision. That preliminary assessment could be conveyed privately to the parties. They could be given an opportunity to present further argument specifically related to the issues which appear likely to control the court's decision. Then, and only then, would the court be sufficiently informed to decide on the equities of the matter.

Whether this suggestion, at any rate in the form here proposed, could be applied in proceedings before the ICJ is problematical. Something of the kind was sought by France and Switzerland in connection with their dispute about the Free Zones. To their Special Agreement of 30 October 1924 submitting the dispute to the PCIJ they added an interpretative note stating that:

> no objection shall be raised on either side to the communication by the Court to the Agents of the Parties, unofficially, and in each other's presence, of any indications which may appear desirable as to the result of the deliberation upon the question formulated in Article 1, paragraph 1, of the Arbitration Convention.[83]

The Court refused to comply with this request, stating that "the spirit and letter of its Statute, in particular Articles 54, paragraph 3,[84] and 58,[85] do not allow the Court 'unofficially' to communicate to the representatives of the two Parties to a case 'the result of the deliberation' upon a question submitted to it for decision; as, in contradiction to that which is permitted by the Rules (Article 32),[86] the Court cannot, on the proposal of the Parties, depart from the terms of the Statute".[87]

In order to alleviate the consequences of its refusal to do all that the Parties had requested, the Court instead inserted in summary form, in the Order that it had been asked to make fixing a period during which the parties were to settle for themselves the new régime to be applied in the Free Zones, its answers to the questions submitted by the parties.

---

[83] For text, see Hudson, *World Court Reports*, vol. II, 453.
[84] "The deliberations of the Court shall take place in private and remain secret."
[85] "The judgment shall be signed by the President and by the Registrar. It shall be read in open Court, due notice having been given to the agents."
[86] "The rules contained under this heading shall in no way preclude the adoption by the Court of such other rules as may be jointly proposed by the parties concerned, due regard being paid to the particular circumstances of each case."
[87] Order, 19 August 1929. The Court emphasized that "special agreements whereby international disputes are submitted to the Court should henceforth be formulated with due regard to the terms in which the Court is to express its opinion according to the precise terms of the constitutional provisions governing its activity, in order that the Court may be able to deal with such disputes in the ordinary course and without resorting, as in the present case, to a construction which must be regarded as strictly exceptional". (PCIJ, Ser. A, No. 22, 13.)

The interpretation that the Court adopted of Articles 54(3) and 58 of its Statute seems unduly restrictive. The action asked of the Court did not have to be seen as infringing upon the privacy and secrecy of the Court's deliberations; nor was it necessary that the "indications" which the Parties sought should have to be construed as the equivalent of a "judgment". Although the same provisions reappear in the same articles of the Statute of the ICJ, it is to be hoped the present Court would approach the matter in a manner more considerate of the wishes of the parties. If the Court's liberal approach to the composition of *ad hoc* chambers is any guide in this connection, this hope may not be disappointed. But even if the ingenuity of parties leads them to devise a formula that would trespass less upon the terms of the Statute than did the words used by France and Switzerland, a doubt must hang over the Court's reaction to this device until such time as it has been further tested in practice or, if the occasion should arise, the Statute has been amended clearly to permit the proposed procedure.

The situation is quite different in the context of *ad hoc* arbitration. Away from the restrictive control of a constitutional text, the Parties are free in formulating an arbitration *compromis* to insert in it almost any procedural instructions they may wish, though it is true that there are some requirements that even an arbitral tribunal should reject as incompatible with the proper discharge of its function.[88] Indeed, there is reason to believe that the idea as stated here[89] has commended itself on at least one occasion to two governments contemplating the submission to

---

[88] P. Weil in "Some Observations on the Arbitral Award in the *Taba Case*", 23 *Israel Law Review* 1 (1989), has drawn attention to the problem that arises when the Parties attempt to constrain an arbitrator by limiting in advance his choice of solutions. He quotes Asser to the effect that "the arbitrator who could only pass judgment in accordance with his instructions [i.e. the *Compromis*] ought, therefore, to have abstained from passing judgment". (*Ibid.*, 20.) The Tribunal in the *Taba Case* did not hesitate to follow the instructions of the Parties. The authorities in Weil's article were not cited to the Tribunal, nor was the following pertinent passage in the *Free Zones* case: "... the Court cannot as a general rule be compelled to choose between constructions determined beforehand none of which may correspond to the opinion at which it may arrive". (PCIJ, Ser. A, No. 22, 5 at 15.)
[89] The suggestion was originally put forward in the author's article on "Equity, Evasion, Equivocation and Evolution in International Law", n. 19 above, 46.

arbitration of a boundary dispute involving the application of equitable principles.[90]

This approach to the procedures applicable in tribunals applying equity or equitable principles is not very different from the procedures that one might expect bodies performing tasks of conciliation and mediation to follow.[91] Thus the ICAO Council in its "Rules for the Settlement of Differences",[92] though distinguishing clearly between the procedures applicable to "disagreements" (the outcome of which can be appealed to the ICJ) and "complaints" (which involve allegations of "injustice or hardship"), nonetheless prescribes as regards the latter an exchange of written pleadings before the Council appoints a committee to consider the complaint. Article 24 of the Rules then provides that the Committee shall call the States concerned into consultation. Thereafter,

> The Committee shall arrange the procedures for the consultation as far as possible in agreement with the parties, and on an informal basis in accordance with the circumstances of each case. It may request additional information and summon representatives of the parties to meet with the Committee at the seat of the Organization or in any other place.

Although there is no express requirement for the Committee to show its report to the parties before it presents it to the Council, it seems implicit in the procedure that the consultation with the parties will necessarily cover the points included in the report.

Nevertheless, the suggestion that such a procedure should be

---

[90] As the arbitration was not pursued, the idea could not be implemented, but there has been no suggestion that the governments concerned have shed their belief in the utility of the idea.

[91] There may be room for investigating in this context the pertinence of the procedures followed by The European Commission on Human Rights in seeking to effect friendly settlement under Article 28 of the European Convention on Human Rights, as well as of the practice followed by the Commission of the European Communities in negotiating with undertakings within the framework of the Community rules on competition.

[92] *ICJ Pleadings, etc., Appeal relating to Jurisdiction of the ICAO Council*, 330.

applied in those bodies that are regarded as primarily judicial or arbitral appears (except for the abortive *Free Zones* precedent) to have about it some elements of novelty. If this is so it is because the problem is relatively new. We have not been faced by it before on anything like its present scale. In grappling with it now we must be ready to introduce innovations in our procedures. Nor should we attempt to escape from the problem by, for example, simply excluding international tribunals from any role in this creative branch of the law. So to do would in effect be to reject an important element in international justice.

If we are to move in the direction of a more flexible and responsive international law, we must do so deliberately; and in full appreciation of what we are doing and of its implications. If political factors in any given multilateral negotiation exclude the formulation of precise rules and lead to what is substantially a prevaricating solution expressed in terms of "equity" (and this is likely to happen more frequently as further multilateral treaties of a sensitive economic character are concluded – particularly in the environmental field), then States must be prepared to accept two things. First, in those situations in which treaty or customary international law requires the parties to seek an agreement on the basis of "equity" or "equitable principles", States will need to be genuinely ready to negotiate seriously and in good faith to implement the obligation thus resting upon them. This may oblige States to develop new attitudes towards negotiation – especially towards the need to compromise – and to explore also the possibility of using new techniques to promote the achievement of their objective. Secondly, States will need to accept that when negotiations have endured beyond the reasonably extended patience of one party, then that party should be entitled to resort for assistance to some form of a tribunal. This help need not necessarily take the form of binding third-party settlement. It could take the form of a conciliation – a process which is inherently not binding. It should, however, be an obligatory process of conciliation which can be initiated by one party alone without the need for further consent by the other. It is, of course, essential that that third person, be he judge or conciliator or mediator, should be someone who is fully involved in the debate with the parties, and that the parties should be equally involved in the debate with him.

It is hardly possible to conceive that the legislature in any democratic society would adopt legislation without debate and without an awareness of all the elements that are relevant to the situation. Why should States and their peoples be prepared to accept less when it comes to law-making through the process of third-party settlement? The judgment, award or recommendation must be one which will command respect – not simply by its recitation of the position of the parties, or its citation of authority, but primarily by the reassurance that it can provide that what really went on in the mind of the arbitrator was reasonable, balanced and impartial rather than unreasoned, capricious and possibly biased.

INDEX

Access to international tribunals, 59-73
Ad hoc judges, 77-78. *See also under* Party-nominated judges
   oath, 80
Administrative tribunals, 13n., 106-7
   appeals from, 106-7
Advisory Committee of Jurists (1920), 51
Advisory Opinions, 4, 16
   substitute for contentious cases, as, 61
   use of, in appeals, 113-14
   whether chambers can give, 95-98
Aggression, 43
Ago, Judge Roberto, 29
Air services agreements, 143
Air transport, 12
Allott, Philip, 6
Alternative dispute resolution, 8
American Convention on Human Rights—
   non-parties, position of—
      —Chile, 30
      —Cuba, 30
      —Paraguay, 30
      —position of, 30
      —United States, 30
American Declaration on Human Rights—
   abortion, 32
   application to non-parties to American Convention, 30-37
      —USA, 31-33
   death penalty, 32
   due process, 33
   equality, 32-33
   Fourth Geneva Convention on Civilians in Time of War, and, 33
   life, right to, 32-33
Amiable compositeur, 136n.
Appeals, 99-116
   administrative tribunals, 106
   basis of—
      —collateral instruments, 104
      —constitutional text, 105
      —original settlement agreement, 101
   contrasted with—
      —interpretation, 100
      —revision, 100
   desirability of, 109-12
   European Commission of Human Rights, from, 107

154 INDEX

European Communities' courts, 108
from national to international courts, 114-16
human rights cases, 107-8
ICSID, 101-4
institutional provision for, 105
Mixed Arbitral Tribunals, from, 104
quasi-judicial decisions, from, 112-14
recourse to—
—another tribunal, 100-5
—original tribunal, 99-100
——under original settlement agreement, 101
Arab-Israeli conflict, 40
Arbitrary results—
avoidance of, 133
Arbitration, 10-13
agreement—
—limitations upon arbitrator's freedom to decide, 149
awards. *See also under* Judgments
—fundamental flaw, 100, 104
—nullity, 100, 104
—preliminary intimations to parties, 149-50
compared with judicial settlement, 85-87, 95
diplomatic process, as, 86-87
Arbitrator-advocate, 81. *See also Ad hoc* judges *and* Party-nominated judges
Arbitrators—
party-nominated, 77-82. *See also* Party-nominated judges
Armed attack, 43
Audi alterem partem rule, 42n.
Aviation, 143

Bantustans. *See* "Homelands"
Bernadotte, Count, 62
Biafra, 60n.
Black, Eugene, 141-42
Bophuthatswana, 60n.
Breaches of the peace, 43

Central American Court of Justice, 15
Chambers of the ICJ, 82-98
advisory opinions, and, 95-98
arbitral or judicial instruments, as, 91-93
criticisms of, 16
increasing use of, 83
intervention applications, 89-90
kinds of, 88
legitimacy of, 90-95

INDEX 155

use of, 88-89
when differing from the full court, 29
Change in the law, 1-2, 48
Channel Islands, 127-30
Ciskei, 41n., 60n.
Claims commissions, 14
Compensation—
  equitable determination, 132
  equitable principles, 135
    —criticisms of, 135
  standards—
    —"full equivalent", 130, 134
    —"just", 134
  valuation distinguished from, 130-1
Compulsory jurisdiction, 15, 25. *See also under* Consent
  chambers of the ICJ, 26-30
  discussion of—
    —in 1920, 25
    —in 1945, 25
  early proposals for, 51
  growing acceptance of, 51
  IACHR, 30-37
  ICJ, and, 23-24
  Law of the Sea Convention (1982), 51
  new approaches to, 48-54
  options, 52
  Security Council—
    —role of, 37-48
Concessions—
  revision of, 137-41
    —arbitral procedure for, 138-41
Conciliation, 6, 7, 8n., 119, 151
  disputes relating to exclusive economic zone, 8
  International Covenant on Civil and Political Rights—
    —Optional Protocol, 8
  UN Rules (1991), 8n.
  Vienna Convention on the Law of Treaties (1969), 7
Conciliation Commission, 70n., 119, 142
Conference on Security and Co-operation in Europe (CSCE), 49
Consent, 48. *See also under* Compulsory jurisdiction
  basis of international jurisdiction, 23
    —weakening of, 23, 48-49, 50-51
  division between theory and practice, 24
  IACHR, in, 30
  ICJ, in, 26-31
  intervention cases, in, 30
  remoteness of, 25
  requirement of—

—reasons for, 24-25
Security Council, and, 37
State conduct—
—implications of, 50
State immunity, and, 54
tenuous, 36-37
Constitutional texts—
interpretation of, 93
Continental shelf, 120
revenue sharing, 120
Corporations—
access to international tribunals, 67-75
—as defendants, 72
—as plaintiffs, 67-72

Decision—
meaning of—
—whether limited to substantive decision, 106
Deep sea mining—
conflicting claims, 144
Dignity of States, 24
Dillard, Judge Hardy, 27
Discounted cash flow. *See* Valuation
Due process, 48
Duties *erga omnes*, 63

Elias, Judge Taslim O., 91
Energy, 12
Environment, 18
Environmental pollution—
liability for—
—enforcement of, 72
Environmental protection—
procedural role of international organizations, 62-64
Equality, 126
Equality of States, 24
Equitable compensation, 130-36
Equitable principles. *See also under* Equity
continental shelf delimitation, 124-30
irrelevant factors—
—access to resources, 127
—relative wealth, 127
—size of parties, 127
meaning of, 117-18
problems in application of, 124-30
uncertainty of, 126
Equitable solution, 142

INDEX 157

Equity, 117-52. *See also* Equitable principles
   application of—
      —according to customary international law, 119, 123-36
      —express request for, 120, 136-45
      —procedural improvements, 147-52
      —procedure for, 146-52
   basis of use of, 119-45
   bodies applying it, 118-19
   compensation cases, in, 130-36
   continental shelf delimitation, in, 124-30
   contra legem, 120n.
   customary international law, and, 123-36
   discretion, and, 132
   ex aequo et bono compared, 118
   ICJ judgments—
      —obscurity in, 125
   judicial discretion, 145-46
   Law of the Sea Convention, and, 120-23
   meaning of, 117-18
   "on the same plane"—
      —views of Fitzmaurice, 126n.
   praeter legem, 120n.
   procedure in application of, 145-52
   reason for use in treaties, 122-23
   secundum legem, 118n.
   treaty, required by, 120
   water resources, allocation of, 136n.
European Communities—
   Commission of, 65
   Court of First Instance, 108
   Court of Justice, 13, 56
   relationship of Community law and international law, 13
European Convention on Human Rights, 13
   recourse to European Court of Human Rights, 107
European Court of Human Rights, 13
European Nuclear Energy Tribunal, 12
Ex aequo et bono, 118, 136-45, 147. *See also under* Equity
Exclusive economic zone—
   conflict resolution, 121
   delimitation, 121

Fair and equitable treatment, 122, 144
Fair market value, 133
Fitzmaurice, Sir Gerald—
   equity, comments on, 125n., 126n., 127n., 129n.
Friendly settlement—
   European Commission of Human Rights, 150n.

GATT, 12
Good offices, 6

Helsinki Rules, 136
"Homelands", 41, 60n.
Hudson, M.O., 118
Human rights—
    enforcement of—
        —available tribunals, 68
        —international organizations, 64-65, 150n.
        —political will, need for, 68
    IACHR, 25, 30-37
    United States, position of, 31

ICSID, 13, 69
    additional facility, 69
    ad hoc committees, 69, 101-3
    —members, 78
    annulment—
        —failure to apply proper law, 102
    annulment procedure, 101-3
    appeals, 101-3
        —incompleteness of system, 103
    banks, non-use by, 69n.
    excess of powers, 102
    nullity—
        —inadequacy of reasons, 103
Illegality of conduct—
    Security Council determination, 42
Individuals—
    access to international tribunals, 67-75
        —as claimants, 67-72
        —as defendants, 72-75
    procedural capacity, 3, 67-75
Inter-American Commission on Human Rights, 13, 25, 30-37
    conduct—
        —implications of, 50
    jurisdiction of—
        —consent to, 30, 33-36
    petitions to, 34
        —relating to USA, 31, 32
    on-site investigations, 36
    organ of the OAS, as, 35
    powers of, 34
    reconsideration of, 33
    Statute of, 34

INDEX

Inter-American Court of Human Rights, 13
International arbitration—
   history of, 14-15
International Civil Aviation Organization, 143
   Council—
     —appeals from, 105
   Rules for the Settlement of Differences, 150
International Coffee Agreements, 12
International Court of Justice, 9-10. *See also* Advisory Opinions, Consent *and* Judgments
   access to—
     —individuals and corporations, by, 67-68
     —international organizations, by, 60-63
   appeal court, as, 112
   appeals to—
     —administrative tribunals, from, 106-7
     —arbitral awards, from, 104
     —ICAO Council, from, 105
   chambers. *See under* Chambers of the ICJ
   compensation, 17
   compulsory jurisdiction. *See* Compulsory jurisdiction
   decisions—
     —process of reaching, 17
   delays, 16
   deliberations, 148-49
     —secrecy of, 148
   dissenting opinions, 91
   interim measures, 4
   intervention. *See* Intervention
   jurisdiction—
     —automatic reservations, 3, 4
     —compulsory, 4
   Optional Clause, 23
     —automatic reservations, 93-95
   powers of, 4
   preliminary observations—
     —frequency of, 50
   references from national courts, 4, 116
   Registry, 16
   Rules (1972), 91
   specialist knowledge, 17
   Statute—
     —Article 34, 3, 4, 59, 66
     —effect of request for preliminary intimation of decision, 149
     —interpretation of, 92-98
     —revision of, 21
   unrecognized States, and, 59n.
   work-load, 16

International courts. *See* International tribunals
International criminal code, 74
International criminal court, 73
International Energy Agency Dispute Settlement Centre, 12
International law—
　customary—
　　—formation of, 32n.
　　—*jus cogens*, 32n.
　　—protest, effect of, 32n.
　equity, whether including, 132
　national courts, in, 115-16
　possibilities of change, 151
International Law Commission, 124-25
　draft code of offences against peace, 73
International Law Reports, 10
International litigation—
　constraints upon, 57
International organizations—
　access to tribunals, 60
　　—as defendants, 65-66
　　—as plaintiffs, 60-65
　administrative tribunals, 13n., 106-7
　commercial arbitrations—
　　—parties to, 61n.
　contentious cases—
　　—standing in, 60n.
　environmental litigation, and, 62-64
　human rights—
　　—enforcement of, 64-65
　procedural capacity, 60-66
　staff—
　　—disputes with, 106-7
International penalties—
　enforcement of, 74
International Prize Court, 115
International Seabed Authority, 121
International Tin Council, 66
International tribunals—
　burden of work, 15
　proliferation of, 9-21
　　—reasons for, 14-22
　size of, considerations affecting, 82-85
　　—functional, 84-85
　　—political, 84
　specialist tribunals, 18
Intervention—
　attitude of States, 30
　consent to, 30

INDEX 161

jurisdictional link, 26, 28
legal interest, 28
non-party, as, 29
party, as, 29
Investments—
  protection of, 68-69
Iran-US Claims Tribunal, 12, 69-70, 130-35, 147
  access by individuals, 70
Iraq, 47
  poison gas—
    —use of, 65
  protest at Security Council action, 44n.
Israel, 47

Jan Mayen Island, 142-43
Jennings, Judge Sir Robert, 29
Jerusalem, 41
Jiménez de Aréchaga, Judge Eduardo, 27-28
Judges—
  fallibility of, 110, 111
  party-nominated, 77-82. *See also* Party-nominated judges
Judgments. *See also under* Arbitration, awards
  interpretation of, 100
  preliminary intimations to parties, 148-49
    —attitude of PCIJ and ICJ, 148-49
  revisions of, 100
Judicial discretion, 48n.
Judicial review. *See* Appeals
Judicial settlement—
  compared with arbitration, 85-87
  national and international contrasted, 7
  nature of, 7
Jurisdiction. *See under* Compulsory jurisdiction
Jus cogens, 7n., 32n.
Justice, administration of—
  defined, 5
Justiciable disputes, 1, 15

Katanga, 40, 47
Kuwait, 41

Lauterpacht, Sir Hersch, 10, 93-95
  An International Bill of the Rights of Man, 3
  Certain Norwegian Loans, 3
  change in international law, and, 2
  Development of International Law, 2

INDEX

Function of Law in the International Community, 1
  international justice, and, 1-5
International Law and Human Rights, 3
  judge of the ICJ, 3-5
  non-justiciable disputes, and, 1
Private Law Sources and Analogies, 1
  Provisional Report on the Revision of the Statute of the ICJ, 4
  South West Africa – Voting Procedure, 3n.
Law of the Sea Convention (1982)—
  conciliation, 7
  continental shelf—
    —revenue sharing, 120
  dispute settlement, 21, 51
  exclusive economic zone, 120, 121, 123
  International Seabed Authority, 121
  landlocked States, 121
  Law of the Sea Tribunal, and, 19-21
  transfer of technology, 122
Law of the Sea Tribunal, 12, 19-22
  access to, 20
    —by international organizations, 61
  competence, 20-21
  composition, 20
  jurisdiction, 20
  parties to disputes before, 20-21
  political origin, 19
  United States, and, 19
Loans—
  revision of, 141-42
London Naval Conference, 115

Mandates, 38n.
McNair, Lord, 10
Mediation, 6
Mixed Arbitral Tribunals, 15
  appeals from, 104
Mixed Claims Commissions, 67

National courts—
  international law in, 114-16
  references to international tribunals, 4, 113-16
National honour, 48
Negotiation, 6, 15
North Moluccas, 60n.
North Sea, 124-27
Nuclear energy—
  patents, 143
    —equitable terms, 143

Nullity—
  declarations by Security Council, 42

Occupied Territories, 41
Oda, Judge Shigeru, 28
Onyeama, Judge Charles, 27, 43-44
Organization of American States, 50. *See also* Inter-American Commission on Human Rights
  General Assembly—
    —powers of, 35
Organization of Eastern Caribbean States, 8n.

"Pariah" States, 47
Party-nominated judges. *See also Ad hoc* judges
  advantages and disadvantages, 78-79
  anomalous position of, 80
  contact with parties, 78n.
  functions of, 80-81
  oath, 79-80
    —desirability of changing, 80-81
  representative quality of, 80
Permanent Court of Arbitration, 14
Permanent Court of International Justice, 15, 148
  appeals to—
    —from Mixed Arbitral Tribunals, 104
Pollution, 12
  dumping, 12
  oil, 12
Procedural standing, 59-73
Procedure—
  adversary—
    —nature of, 146
  equity, in application of, 145-52
Protest—
  effect of, 32n.

Quasi-judicial bodies, 37-48
  General Assembly, 38
  Security Council, 37-48
Quasi-judicial decisions—
  appeals against, 112-14

Railways—
  revision of concessions, 137
Recourse. *See under* Appeals
Red Cross, 65
References—
  from national to international courts, 113-15

—EEC Treaty, Article 177, 116
Rhodesia. *See* Southern Rhodesia
Root —Phillimore plan, 84

Schwebel, Judge Stephen, 29n.
Scilly Islands, 129, 147
Security Council—
    determinations—
        —of fact, 43
        —of law, 43
    due process in, 48
    judicial control of, 39
    jurisdiction of—
        —quasi-judicial competence, 37
    nature of, 42
    peace-keeping organ, as, 39
    Peace Treaty with Italy—
        —functions under, 47n.
    permanent members of—
        —position of, 37n.
    powers of, 39
        —compared with national organs, 39
        —*re* compulsory jurisdiction of ICJ, 52-53
        —source of, 46
    President of—
        —Statement (1979), 41n.
    procedure, 42
        —resolutions of, 42
        —summary quality, 49
    protest against conduct of, 44
    quasi-judicial activities, 42-43
        —consent to, 46
    recourse against decisions of, 113-14
    resolutions—
        —absence of reasoning, 43
        —adoption, method of, 42-43
        —attitude of members, 44
        —binding force, 45, 53
        —declarations of illegality, 44
        —determinations of law, 39-42
        —distinguished from individual acts of members, 45
        —effect of, 45
        —interpretation of, 45
        —nature of, 45
        —types of, 44
        —whether a court, 44
Security Council Resolutions—
    —9 (1946), 60n.

—S/5002 (1961), 40n.
—216 (1965), 40n.
—217 (1965), 40n.
—232 (1966), 40n.
—252 (1968), 41n.
—253 (1968), 40n.
—276 (1970), 40n.
—277 (1970), 40
—298 (1971), 41n.
—478 (1980), 41n.
—662 (1990), 41n.
Sette-Camara, Judge José, 28
Shahabuddeen, Judge Mohamed, 90-96
South Africa, 47
South West Africa, 40
Southern Rhodesia, 40, 47
Special tribunals—
   significance of, 52
   use of, 17-22
State immunity, 54-57
   abolition of, 56
   acts *jure imperii*, 55
   basis of, 55
   consent, and, 54-57
   human rights, and, 56
State succession—
   property, division of—
      —equitable proportions, 136n.
States—
   compared with individuals, 24
   unrecognized States—
      —access to ICJ, 59n.
Steyern, N. von, 141
Stuyt, A.M., 14

Taiwan, 60n.
Tarassov, Judge, 90, 91
Threats to the peace, 43
Transfer of technology, 122
Transkei, 60
Travaux préparatoires, 92
   Statute of the ICJ, of, 27
Treaties—
   arbitral settlement, for, 11-12
   interpretation of. *See also Travaux préparatoires*
      —intention of draftsmen, 92
   Vienna Convention (1969), 7
Tribunals, composition of, 77-98

Trieste, 47n.
Turkish Republic of Northern Cyprus, 41, 47, 60n.

United Nations—
    Charter—
        —consent, as source of, 46
    Decade of International Law, 49
    General Assembly—
        —quasi-judicial body, as, 38
        —powers of, 38, 38n.
        —Resolution 2145 (XXI), 44
        —resolutions, 3n.
    Human Rights Committee, 8, 13
    non-members, position of, 47
    Secretary-General—
        —statement of 10 January 1947, 46n.
    Security Council. *See* Security Council *and* Security Council Resolutions
    succession to League of Nations, 38n.
United Nations Environment Programme, 63
United States of America—
    IACHR—
        —on-site investigations, 36
        —participation in, 32
    Senate of—
        —Advice on Buenos Aires Protocol, 36
Upper Silesian Arbitral Tribunal, 67n.
Ushant, 129, 147

Valletta Principles for Dispute Settlement (1991), 49n.
Valuation—
    as objective process, 130-36
    compensation distinguished from, 130-31
    discounted cash flow (DCF), 131, 132
    fair market value, 133
Vance, Cyrus—
    IACHR—
        —endorsement of, 36
Venda, 41n., 60n.
Vessels, prompt release of, 21
Vienna Convention on the Law of Treaties (1969). *See* Treaties
Vital interests, 48

Waldock, Judge Sir Humphrey, 27
War crimes—
    trials for, 73
Water resources, 135
Westlake, John, 5
World Bank Centre for the Settlement of Investment Disputes. *See* ICSID